THE
METROPOLITAN
LINE

THE METROPOLITAN LINE

LONDON'S FIRST UNDERGROUND RAILWAY

CLIVE FOXELL CBE, FREng

The History Press

Frontispiece: 'drawing of Met locos' (*Met Publicity*)

TO SHIRLEY AND ELIZABETH

Other railway histories by the author:

Chesham Shuttle (1996)
Chesham Branch Album (1998)
Story of the Met & GC Joint Line (2000)
Memories of the Met & GC Joint Line (2002)
Rails to Metro-Land (2005)

'I have only made a nosegay of culled flowers, and have brought nothing of my own but the thread that ties them together' - Montaigne

First published 2010

The History Press
The Mill, Brimscombe Port
Stroud, Gloucestershire, GL5 2QG
www.thehistorypress.co.uk

Reprinted 2010

British Library Cataloguing in Publication Data.
A catalogue record for this book is available from the British Library.

ISBN 978 0 7524 5396 5

Typesetting and origination by The History Press
Printed in Great Britain

CONTENTS

PREFACE

The now seemingly insignificant Metropolitan Railway can claim to have had an influence on the haphazard evolution of our railway system out of all proportion to its tracks, reaching just 47 miles from London. However, it was the first underground passenger railway which was embraced by the notorious Victorian entrepreneur Sir Edward Watkin as part of his machinations for an ambitious plan to create an intercontinental railway, and when this scheme collapsed following his death the Met became embroiled with another of his companies (the Great Central Railway) in a joint company.

Unfortunately Watkin had bequeathed to the Met a line through lovely countryside, but with few passengers to generate revenue. Nevertheless, his successor at the Met, Robert Selbie turned this to advantage by creating *Metro-land* and thus financial success. Finally in 1933 it lost its identity on being reluctantly absorbed by London Transport and subsequently became a key part of the ongoing saga of railway nationalisation and privatisation. Somewhat surprisingly, interest in the Metropolitan Railway has actually grown, probably from recognition of its role in attempting to create this Arcadian form of commuting suburbia known as *Metro-land*, and immortalised by the works of Sir John Betjeman.

There was a period where the proclaimed attributes of *Metro-land* – namely living in an ordered countryside with easy access to London – were derided. However, not only is the area still highly regarded, but as journey times improve with the new trains *Metro-land* is moving to beyond Aylesbury.

As a boy I was fortunate to witness the last throes of the Met, then, as a teenager during the Second World War, to serve as a casual cleaner at the Neasden (London & North Eastern Railway) engine shed, and afterward commute from Chesham for many years. These experiences, together with my researches, have led me to write this book which tries to meld the characters with the social and political pressures that have combined to produce such a chaotic environment for the evolution of the railways in this country and why, in spite of this, the Met conjures up such interest. Indeed, it has been the efforts of a few managers together with the resilience of many of those who operate the railways that has led to any progress.

The frenzied story of the Met is a fascinating blend of a great variety of trains, idiosyncratic operating methods and sheer nostalgia.

Clive Foxell, spring 2010

ACKNOWLEDGEMENTS

The main sources for this book are listed, but have been supplemented by my own research based on the Met records variously held at the London Metropolitan Archive, the Public Record Office, 55 Broadway, London's Transport Museum and the Buckinghamshire Record Office. My thanks are due to the kindness of the staff involved. Another important aspect has been the personal recollections provided by ex-Met staff from Signalman Tony Geary, Iris Prior a Ticket Office clerk in the Second World War, to the late John Parnham of the Civil Engineers. I am most grateful for their efforts.

For reasons of rarity I have had to use a few illustrations that may be familiar to illustrate some early scenes. Otherwise I have attempted to find an eclectic selection of less well-known ones that not only illustrate the narrative and evoke the varied and particular nature of the Met, but that also reflect the changing social background.

Regrettably with time some who had already contributed photographs to my previous works, such as C.R.L. Coles, Geoff Gamble, Stephen Gradidge, John Parnham, Ron Potter and J.J. Smith have passed on. I particularly wish to thank Peter Green, the well-known railway artist, and other stalwarts who have provided illustrations including David Bosher, Richard Casserley, R.S. Carpenter, Jean Caterine, John Gerchen, Richard Hardy, Roger Marks, Simon Murphy (London's Transport Museum Photo Archive), Les Reason, Albin Reed, Rodney Sedgewick, H.F. Wheeler, Ron White (Colour Rail), Dewi Williams, Tom Samuels (UK Aerial Photos), Sarah Williams (Museum of London) and the many others who have contributed. In the case of 'orphan works', where the ownership is confused or unknown, I have performed the suggested diligent searches. In trying to acknowledge the sources of all the illustrations, I give my apologies where the attributions are incorrect.

My sincere thanks also go to Elizabeth Foxell, Len Bunning and Peter Cowan who have reviewed my drafts for errors; any remaining are my own responsibility. As it happened I became ill during the writing of this book, and I wish to thank Emily Locke and her colleagues at The History Press for their support, encouragement and professionalism in turning my work into reality.

INTRODUCTION

This book attempts to explain how the small Metropolitan Railway, initially less than 4 miles long, came to be a significant factor in the development of railways in Britain. Due to a variety of factors, ranging from its strategic situation to becoming intertwined with the Great Central Railway, it then evolved through the saga of various mergers into British Railways and its present-day successors. To follow this tortuous story it is relevant to include the wider social, political and economic factors that have drastically influenced events.

NOTE ON THE TEXT

In this book, the Metropolitan Railway is referred to as the 'Met', the Met & GC Joint Committee as the Met & GCJ, and the phases within the various forms of London Transport as 'LT', until succeeded by Transport for London, 'TfL'.

CHAPTER ONE

THE EVOLUTION OF THE RAILWAYS IN BRITAIN

The growth of railways in relation to other forms of transport, from turnpike roads to motorways, is summarised in the diagram on page 11. One is struck by the similar exponential growth of *all* modes of transport, even the building of the early canals, followed by a maturity reaching a plateau as users moved to a newer mode of travel. Interestingly, most forms of technology that satisfy the customers' needs develop in the same pattern, as with communications for example, from the telegraph, telephone, internet, to broadband. But the factors that influenced the evolution of the railways in this country, with particular reference to the Met, may be summarised as follows:

1830-1900: ENTREPRENEURS AND OWNERS

Following the success of Stephenson's Liverpool & Manchester Railway, Britain was among the first in the world to exploit rail transport, as here builders promoted new lines in unruly profusion. The turmoil of this phase is illustrated by the map of the railways that were *not* built in Buckinghamshire (see page 12), for in the area covered by this book some ninety lines were planned (equal to some 3,000 miles), of which only some twenty-four were actually built (634 miles). Of the latter, virtually all except the Aylesbury & Buckingham Railway (A&BR) were promoted by the first nearby mainlines, the Great Western Railway (GWR) and London & Birmingham Railway.

In general, most expansion came from this type of dominant railway company, plus the activities of a few major financiers and entrepreneurs. Of the latter, Sir Edward Watkin was a classic example who changed the course of the Met and later created the last mainline, the Great Central Railway (GCR). However, the 'rush for rail' was seriously disrupted by the Parliamentary approval process plus a cyclical lack of funding due to caution arising from 'railway mania', banking crises, economic downturns and wars.

1901-1922: CONSOLIDATION AND WAR

Having built most of the railway network, the emphasis of the numerous railway companies focused on maximising the financial returns on the investment, growing revenue by improving services and efficiency. A forced collaboration during the First World War demonstrated the advantages of rationalisation and so the post-war government 'grouped' most of the railways into four new companies. However, in practice the war had significantly weakened the railways as the Government failed to adequately recompense them for their efforts and indirectly encouraged the widespread competitive use of motor transport as well as stimulating trade union activity.

1923-1947: GROUPING AND WAR

Following this grouping into the 'Big Four' railway companies they were mainly concerned with integrating their constituents, but soon the country was beset by the serious General Strike and a world depression. The 1930s saw some economic recovery and the railways tried to maintain the status quo in the face of growing competition from cars and lorries until being overtaken by the Second World War.

1948-1996: NATIONALISATION (BRITISH RAILWAYS)

This time the war badly damaged the railway infrastructure, both by bombing and by lack of upkeep. Yet again inadequate payment for their wartime services further weakened the run-down railway companies, and with a new Labour government nationalisation was inevitable. But lack of clear objectives and investment, combined with a Byzantine bureaucracy, left British Railways (BR) relatively ineffective against competition from the ongoing spread of motor transport.

1997 ONWARDS: SEMI-PRIVATISATION

One of the last acts of a weakening Conservative administration was to privatise BR, albeit as a financial private/government hybrid. Whilst the private train operating companies have performed reasonably with subsidies, the private infrastructure contractors have performed poorly, with the overarching Network Rail/Railtrack virtually reduced to a 'shell' trying to manage an array of contracts. The result has been a structure of labyrinthine complexity trying to operate under Government indecision and underinvestment at a time of growth in demand.

Perhaps because Britain was among the first to adopt rail transport it explored many different routes in developing a national system, whilst other countries learnt from our experiences. However, it is apparent even from this outline that the evolution of the railways in this country has been more influenced not just by the behaviour of the companies themselves, but even more by events and pressures largely outside of their control. These include wars, political and governmental actions, the economic situation and many other seemingly unrelated forces that individually, or together, have seriously affected the outcomes.

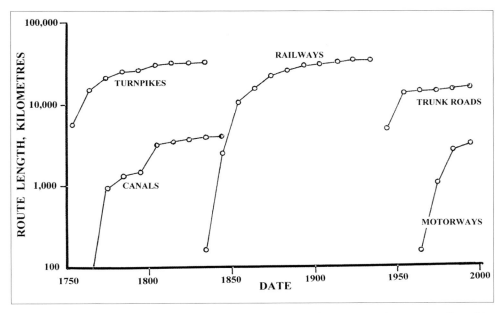

The similarity in the rate of evolution of the successive forms of transport in the UK, as indicated by route length. (*Department of Transport*)

The railways were one of the first examples of capitalisation on a large scale, and we are only just beginning to understand how unpredictable influences can cause such a system to become unmanageable. It seems that in any such system where its state evolves with time the dynamics are highly sensitive to its initial conditions (sometimes called the 'butterfly effect'), and become not just random but deterministically chaotic. Other classic examples of this behaviour are that of the weather and the financial markets, where extreme events are difficult to predict. The future of the railways can be seen as just another case of a complex system reacting in a manner determined largely by the initial conditions. This story of the Met and the Met & GCJ is littered with examples of this type of unpredictability. Two maxims follow from the laws of chaos. First is the so-called 'Law of Unintended Consequences', in which an unexpectedly good ('windfall') or poor ('bad luck') outcome can occur.

An example of a surprisingly positive benefit would be Watkin's Folly, a tower which was built by Sir Edward in his pleasure gardens at Wembley to rival that of Eiffel's in Paris and which proved to be a costly failure. But the large site later generated substantial profits for the Met as the location for the 1924/5 Wembley Exhibition and also for a major *Metro-land* housing development. An illustration of a negative outcome would be the consequences of the new Metropolitan Railway, built to ease traffic in the City, which was so successful that it attracted people into London!

The second maxim is 'history never (quite) repeats itself', for it follows that most comparisons with past events involve misconceptions about the present and an impoverished view of the past, and so looking to the past for guidance is problematical.

BUCKINGHAMSHRE RAILWAYS

PLANNED, BUT NOT BUILT 1845 – 1890

(After F Cockman Records of Bucks Vol 19 p156)

The chaotic evolution of the railways in Buckinghamshire between 1845 and 1890, showing the sixty-six lines some 2,736 miles long that were planned, *but not built*. Only twenty-four railways were actually constructed, totalling 634 miles, and these were dominated by the Great Western and London & North Western Railways. (*C.A.F Coll*)

However, even with this better understanding of these pitfalls, with the surfeit of factors that can influence the success or otherwise of a major railway system there is no easy way to distil them into an appropriate course of action. In reality, most organisations do not last very long before failing or metamorphosing by sale or merger into something different. Few are fortunate enough to be run by someone who has clear basic objectives, who takes a measured view of change and who yet is prepared to be flexible in the light of real trends.

Of those leaders who have influenced the Met and its associates in this positive manner the list would probably include Charles Pearson (City Solicitor), Sir Edward Watkin (Met & GCR), Sir Sam Fay (GCR), Robert Selbie (Met), Frank Pick (LT), Sir Bob Reid (British Railways) and Adrian Shooter (Chiltern Railways). Appropriately it was Pick who said that 'an organisation is more dependent on its leader than its structure'.

The rest of this book describes the evolution of the Met and its associates against the volatile background, the influence of these people and how much of their future remains just as unpredictable.

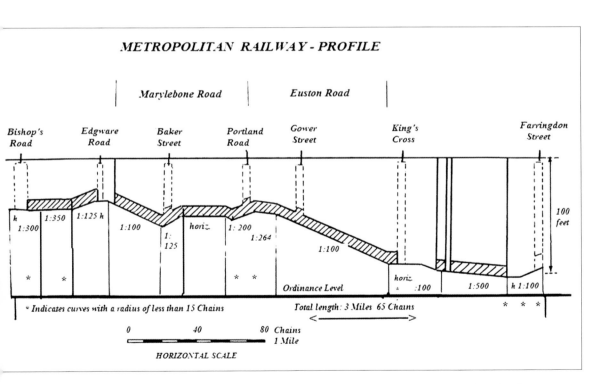

Initially, the Metropolitan Railway ran from Paddington to Farringdon, being mainly built under the New Road, which had also been created by Charles Pearson. This shows the gradient profile of the line. (*C.A.F. Coll after The Engineer, 17/07/1895*)

Most of the Met was built by navvies first excavating a trench down the New Road. In this, an eight-layer brick arch was built to form a tunnel for the railway and then the road was re-laid over it, giving the technique the name of 'cut and cover'. (*National Museum of Science & Industry*)

Even after the opening of the initial Metropolitan Railway, the congestion of the horse-drawn traffic continued for a while. However, even Watkin used such omnibuses, as shown in the centre, as a temporary link for passengers between his Metropolitan and South Eastern Railways (*LTM*)

THE FIRST UNDERGROUND PASSENGER RAILWAY

Many of the early proposals for constructing new railways suffered from an excess of enthusiasm, which led to failure when the commercial realities became apparent. However, the building of the Metropolitan Railway arose from the real need to solve the problem of the rapidly growing amount of traffic clogging the streets of Victorian London. The Industrial Revolution had brought many more workers into the City who were increasingly forced to look for places to live on the periphery. Many people walked to work, often long distances. Their homes were being built on land that had provided much of the food for London, but now this had to be brought in from much further afield. The conveyance of such provisions, together with other materials and the people who lived and worked in the City, was almost entirely by horse.

Add to this the transport by horse-drawn cab and omnibus and by 1860 there were about 300,000 horses stabled in London (together with those visiting), which themselves added to the traffic with the need to bring large volumes of provender for their feed and to remove an estimated 300,000 tons of manure per year. Such was the shortage of space that many of the larger stables were multi-storey.

In addition, with the main markets being in the City, by 1850 about 2.5 million cattle, sheep, pigs and even ducks were driven from many miles away, through London to the abattoirs. One can easily imagine the congestion caused by such herds of animals converging with the existing horse-drawn traffic which was bringing London to a standstill. This had been a cause for concern for some time but no realistic solutions had emerged. However a persuasive, persistent and influential campaigner emerged in the 1830s in the shape of Charles Pearson, the Solicitor to the City, ably supported by the City Surveyor, John Stevens.

Pearson was driven by the desire to improve the lot of the workers in London and he rebuilt many of the appalling roads and sewers. In parallel, the new trunk railways were developing at a rapid pace, with termini being restricted by law from the 1840s to the then outskirts of London; it was impractical to consider widespread demolition of the more expensive of the densely packed buildings to make way for a railway. However, against all prophecies of 'hell and damnation', to those travelling by train underground ever-longer tunnels (e.g. the 3-mile-long Woodhead Tunnel of 1845) were being shown to be feasible, albeit involving tremendous engineering efforts.

Against this background Pearson encouraged proposals for an underground railway linking the termini to the north of London, but progress was continually delayed by the inevitable problems of financing, Parliamentary approval and the vagaries of the economic situation. However, Pearson did succeed in inspiring the influential businessman William Mallins, who was associated with the very successful railway contractors Samuel Peto and Thomas Brassey, to launch the North Metropolitan Railway to run underneath the New Road connecting the railway termini.

A Parliamentary committee was supportive and the necessary Act was passed in 1853. The company was re-formed as the Metropolitan Railway and the required finance

Pearson had intended that the Met, as well reducing road congestion, would also provide a link between the railway termini along his New Road. This drawing shows the junction between the main Met dual tracks and on the left the link with the Great Northern Railway at King's Cross. The Met tracks include broad-gauge rails for the GWR trains. (The Builder)

After a successful inspection in December 1862, followed by rehearsals to train the staff, on 9 January 1863 the Met was formally opened with a banquet held in Farringdon Station. The platforms were boarded over for some 700 guests to celebrate in the traditional manner. (*Illustrated London News*)

of £800,000 was eventually raised, mainly by Pearson from the City Corporation (£200,000) and eventually £175,000 from the GWR who needed to get rail access from Paddington to the City. Nevertheless, they made it a condition that a third rail be laid to accommodate their different broad-gauge trains.

The eminent Sir John Fowler was appointed engineer, but delegated the crucial tunnelling work to Benjamin Baker who employed a 'cut and cover' technique for the underground sections. In this, from Praed Street a large trench was dug – mainly just below the New Road – with walls and an arched roof built with eight layers of bricks. Major difficulties with subsidence had to be overcome as well as flooding from the River Fleet sewer on the line to Farringdon.

Whilst this work proceeded Fowler tackled the prime concern of potential passengers, namely their difficulty of breathing in the smoke-filled tunnels which would be created by the numerous steam locomotives. To solve this he devised a locomotive, built by Robert Stephenson, in which the steam was generated in the engine by pre-heated bricks inserted in the firebox during pauses at the stations. This so-called *Fowler's Ghost* failed during tests and the trial workings were hauled by the conventional engines of the contractors. However, these confirmed the serious problems of smoke choking the underground travellers.

Fortunately the GWR were growing anxious about their investment and getting passengers into central London so their Locomotive Superintendent, Sir Daniel Gooch, came to the aid of the Met by building some improvised 'condensing' locomotives, in which their exhaust was passed out through the cold water in the tanks of the locomotive. Thus the Met opened on 10 January 1863, with GWR broad-gauge locomotives and coaches successfully carrying

With the failure of *Fowler's Ghost* and the breakdown of relations with the GWR, in desperation the Met turned to Beyer Peacock to supply suitable engines. They modified an existing design intended for Portugal, as shown above, to which Burnett of the Met added condensing apparatus to reduce pollution underground. (*C.A.F. Coll*)

In spite of all the predictions of suffocation and damnation that had been heaped on the first underground passenger railway, the Met was a great success with all Londoners, from artisans to the aristocracy. This scene at Moorgate, with one of the new Met Class A tank engines in the background, conveys something of the popularity. (*ILN*)

40,000 passengers that day. Unfortunately, Pearson did not live to see his ideas brought to fruition, but the Met awarded his widow an annuity of £250.

Underground travel became very popular with those in the City, with 9,455,168 passengers being carried at a profit of £101,707 in the first year. In the following year, they recognised the advantages of attracting 'workmen' to use early trains and offered a cheap return for 3*d* rather than the normal 9*d*, which substantially increased their profits. However, the first of what was to become a series of confrontations occurred in 1863 when the GWR became reluctant to increase the frequency of trains to meet the Met's needs and this led to the GWR withdrawing their trains, hoping to force the Met to abandon the idea.

The Met was saved by the Great Northern Railway who loaned some of their engines, modified with condensers by Archibald Sturrock – otherwise there would have been no trains for five years! Looking for a permanent solution the Met turned to the Beyer Peacock Company which was making some 4-4-0 tank engines for export to the Tudela & Bilbao Railway in Spain, which Robert Burnett was able to convert with condensers. Delivered in 1868, these Class A engines saved the situation, hauling standard-gauge trains over the Met well into the next century!

As a result of this success the Met extended east to Moorgate (1865) and Aldgate (1876), west to South Kensington (1868) – and, in conjunction with the GWR (friends again!), to Hammersmith (1864). The completion of an Inner Circle line was bedevilled by disagreements with the competing Metropolitan & District Railway (M&DR) who were building the section beside the new Embankment. Nevertheless, with an Inner Circle in prospect, Met seemed set to prosper.

Reflecting the spread of the Met, here Met Class A tank No.46 is seen at Edgware Road waiting to depart for New Cross via the East London Line and the Brunel tunnel under the River Thames. (*K. Bennest / London Underground Railway Society*)

An independent company was behind building a branch from Baker Street to Swiss Cottage. In view of the gradients involved, Burnett of the Met produced some powerful engines, but it was found that the Class A tanks could easily cope and so his locomotives were sold to the Taff Vale Railway. They added the cab shown below to protect the footplate crew from the weather. (*Locomotive & General Railway Photographs*)

CHAPTER TWO

THE RISE AND FALL OF
SIR EDWARD WATKIN

ON BECOMING PART OF WATKIN'S EMPIRE

With John Parson as chairman, the Met had demonstrated that underground passenger railways were practical and profitable. The Met certainly appeared to flourish, with passenger numbers quadrupling by 1870 and dividends reaching 7 per cent. However, some shareholders became so concerned about the accounting practices that were producing these apparently good results that they took successful legal actions on the appropriateness of various valuations, definition of incomes, and effectively paying dividends out of capital.

After a tumultuous half-yearly meeting in 1872 Parson was forced to concede to reforming the Board and, as a result, a group of Manchester-based directors proposed appointing a fellow Mancunian – Sir Edward Watkin – to the Board. After a seemly pause he accepted the invitation and, being a successful leading railway figure, soon became chairman - but little did the shareholders of the Met realise what plans Watkin had in mind for their small company!

From a modest background, Watkin had become interested in municipal, political and liberal matters, but impending marriage forced him to find a job. Fortuitously, in 1845 a friend found him a position as secretary of the Trent Valley Railway (TVR) and this brought out all his latent instincts for concentration, hard work and managerial ability, to the extent that they almost became an obsession. It was lucky that the TVR would become vital to the interests of the huge London & North Western Railway (LNWR), and their notorious manager, Capt. Mark Huish, soon acquired the TVR on mutually beneficial terms to Watkin, who then joined Huish.

This was the start of Watkin's self-made career, and, although we are primarily concerned with his subsequent extensive railway interests, he did have a wider concern for transport furthering international trade. Thus he travelled widely, running overseas ventures such as the Grand Trunk Railway across Canada and the Hudson Bay Company. But he also saw political power as the way to influence these matters and became a Liberal MP for a period of some forty-two years as well as a confidant of Gladstone.

Such was his reputation that the Government often asked his assistance on matters ranging from introducing the Dominion of Canada to sorting out the logistics in the Crimean War. Almost secondary to this was his being chairman or director of the Manchester, Sheffield & Lincolnshire Railway (MS&LR) – and some twenty other railway companies. So, obviously here was a man of experience and calibre who could save the Met.

Baker St Station.

The original Met station at Baker Street was little more than stairways leading to the platforms below. With the increasing traffic, boosted by the opening of the adjacent Bakerloo deep tube in 1906, the buildings were suitably upgraded. Selbie would later replace them by magnificent headquarters, flats and shops worthy of the Met. (*C.A.F. Coll*)

The original Met line was extended to the East, and also the West in conjunction with the GWR as the Hammersmith & City line. In order to serve the major Franco-British Exhibition at the White City in 1908, a new station was opened at Wood Lane, as shown above. (*C.A.F. Coll*)

Watkin pushed the Met through the North-West of London in stages until reaching Rickmansworth in 1887. The line had a sharp curve to avoid an uncooperative landowner which caused a speed restriction of 15mph. It also necessitated the very tall posts to make the signals visible to the train crews. Watkin then considered alternative routes on through High Wycombe or Amersham, but instead decided to go through Chesham and join the LNWR at Tring. (*Ray East*)

The line to Chesham dropped down the valley of the River Chess at 1 in 60 to terminate at The Moor (above) on the outskirts of the town. However, Watkin persuaded the inhabitants to give £2,000 to build the railway on into the town. Here the embankment is under construction, leaving the adjacent new Railway Hotel isolated. (*Ray East*)

In 1888 the line to Chesham had to drop down into the Chess Valley at 1 in 66, which involved major embankments and cuttings through the chalk. This is the site of Chesham Station when the contractor, Firbank, gave a short trip for some of the leading contributors who had paid for the line to come into the centre of the town. (*Ray East*)

Having been thwarted in extending the Chesham line to Tring (and the LNWR), Watkin diverted the Met mainline north from Chalfont Road in 1892, thus leaving Chesham on a branch line. Here a new train for Aylesbury is approaching Chalfont Road, where initially coaches for Chesham were detached, but this was soon replaced by the Shuttle service. (*C.A.F. Coll*)

Watkin was also thwarted on his route through Amesham by the local landowners – the Tyrwhitt-Drakes – and had to build the line over higher land to the north. However, he had the last laugh as a larger new town developed around his Met station and the inhabitants of the 'old' town needed to use a horse bus to reach the trains. (*Ray East*)

Edward VII used the Met and subsequently the GCR for rendezvous at his friend's establishments in Bucks. The scheduling and timekeeping of these trains was the cause of much friction between the two railway companies. Here in 1907 and bound for Alfred Rothschild at Halton, the GCR Royal train with the royal 4-lamp code approaches Amersham, headed by a new Robinson class 8D 4-4-2 locomotive, no.364 *Lady Henderson*. (*R. Hardy*)

Having pushed the Met to Aylesbury in 1892, Watkin acquired the A&BR to Quainton Road and got Firbank to upgrade the light track to mainline standards. Always on the outlook for extra traffic, he also took over the Duke of Buckingham's estate tramway to Brill. Above one of the decrepit O&AT engines: *Wotton* No.2 at Brill. (*Ken Nunn-LCGB*)

The trains intended for the underground Inner Circle, now handled most of the services to the extremities of the line. Still without a cab to protect the crew, Class A 4-4-0T No.44 heads an equally venerable train of rigid four- and eight-wheeled carriages near Northwood. This was one of the many places where a footpath crossed the lines! (*Ken Nunn/Locomotive Club of Great Britain*)

Quickly taking complete control by making one of his MS&LR henchmen, John Bell, company secretary, he soon restored confidence. But there were other aspects to Watkin that were later to be revealed to the unsuspecting shareholders. Firstly, he was very secretive about his true objectives, often taking short-term actions that might prove to be useful later. Secondly, like a chameleon, as circumstances required he could switch from being affable, statesman-like and loyal to being argumentative, over-bearing, vindictive, and litigious, even reneging on agreements.

It was this negative characteristic that soon became apparent, for Watkin, as chairman of the South Eastern Railway (SER), was already locked in a bitter dispute with John Staats Forbes of the London Chatham & Dover Railway (LC&DR) over the lucrative traffic to the Channel ports. Unfortunately he now widened this antagonism to embrace the relations between the Met and Forbes's other company, the Metropolitan District Railway (MDR). This delayed the completion and operation of the Inner Circle line for years.

Also, the unsuspecting Met shareholders did not realise that Watkin saw their Met as a vital piece in his bigger railway jigsaw. By joining the MS&LR, SER and Chemin de Fer du Nord, he could create a railway from his home at Manchester to Paris – which held a particular attraction to him for trade and other reasons. Watkin had realised whilst the Met was essentially a short line in central London it had just acquired two vestigial branches that that would facilitate his objective.

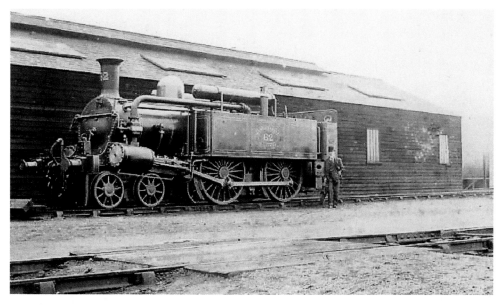

Watkin was always interested in technical innovations, particularly in those that could improve the performance of his railways. He encouraged the early trials of electrification and, in 1898, the above experimental conversion to oil burning of Class A engine No.62 with Holden's apparatus. But it was expensive and emitted too much smoke. (*C.A.F. Coll*)

To replace the hired engines used by the A&BR, in 1894/5 the Met got Sharp Stewart to build some light 2-4-0 tank engines (Class D). Unfortunately, they were not a success and after working passenger trains beyond Aylesbury, they ended their days relegated to the occasional goods turn. Here is a rare picture of No.76 near Wendover. (*Ken Nunn – LCGB*)

Near the end of Watkin's reign, in 1898 a typical Met mainline down train of the period to Verney Junction passes the footpath crossing at Northwood. Headed by Class E 4-4-0T No.68, a milk van is followed by a standard Ashbury rigid eight-wheeled 5-coach set and a four-wheeled coach. (L&GRP)

An up goods train from Quainton Road, running downhill towards Rickmansworth. Another Class E tank, No. 33, heads a load of mainly coal wagons but which also includes a typical sight of that time, with a cattle wagon liberally covered in a white lime wash to act as a disinfectant. (*John Gerchen Coll*)

To the north the Met had encouraged a branch to Swiss Cottage and beyond, whilst to the south it had acquired, as the receiver, the moribund East London Railway under the River Thames via Brunel's pioneering tunnel. This would enable Watkin to link with his SER route to Folkestone. Thus, in Watkin's bold strategy he aimed to extend his MS&LR south through the Midlands to join a Met Extension from London, and build a Channel Tunnel to link his English and French railways to access Paris.

Actions towards this end were only revealed to shareholders (and even colleagues!) in small palatable steps, often camouflaged by euphemistic generalisations such as 'the need to break out of London to avoid the constraints of competitors'. Ironically, to fund this expansion programme, he employed some of the same dubious practices that he had condemned on coming to the Met, but his confidence and charisma usually carried the day. Equally, large investors often became so committed that they could not afford to pull out. Thus, Watkin's plans for the Met were motivated by his mainline ambitions, rather than those of the Met shareholders.

So the Met was extended north-west in stages through Neasden to Harrow (1880), Rickmansworth (1887), and then Chesham (1889). Although this may now seem somewhat surprising at that time Chesham was not an unreasonable destination as, with a population of some 6,500, it was one of the larger towns in Buckinghamshire. But Watkin's real motivation was to then join the LNWR at Tring to gain ready access to the north. However, this move failed and the Met was extended out to Aylesbury (1892), and thence by acquisition of the Duke of Buckingham's Aylesbury & Buckingham Railway (A&BR) reached Quainton Road in 1897 – some 44 miles from London.

From the north, by 1898 the MS&LR was extended south from the Midlands coalfields to meet the Met and hopefully run over its line to Baker Street. This new mainline was built to the highest standards reflecting Watkin's continental ambitions. In parallel, he tackled the remaining gap in his scheme by starting to excavate the first tunnel under the English Channel in 1881. The scale of his Francophile ambitions was also shown by his commencing of the construction of a tower – rather higher than the Eiffel – near the Met at Wembley, in 1894.

As the MS&LR was extended southward to join the Met even Watkin came to admit that the Inner Circle was already near full capacity, and so he started to consider duplicating the existing tunnels. Equally Baker Street Station would not be able to cope with the extra traffic and so he decided to build a line for the MS&LR trains, branching from the Met at Finchley Road to a grand new station at Marylebone. His plans now included a further line for through trains to join the Inner Circle near Edgware Road, thus enabling them to travel via his Channel Tunnel to the Continent. Needless to say the massive works at Marylebone raised strong protests from the current residents, particularly his sacrilegious tunnels under Lord's Cricket Ground, but Watkin deployed all his usual methods of persuasion, aggression, charm and of spending the MS&LR's money to win round the objectors.

Watkin's Channel Tunnel was excavated for some 2,000 yards from both of the English and French coasts, whilst suffering severe criticism from the British Army in that it would render this country more likely to be invaded. So in 1891 the British Government closed the workings, shown above when the present Channel Tunnel cut into them. (*Nick Catford*)

Whilst Watkin's Channel Tunnel was in trouble, other parts of his 'dream' were also disintegrating. The animosity between the Met and the GCR had forced the GCR to negotiate a joint route with the GWR to bypass the Met. This 1903 scene encapsulates the situation with this new line joining the old route at Neasden. In the background, the tower now known as 'Watkin's Folly', has been abandoned due to subsidence. (*Record Office of Leicestershire, Leicester & Rutland*)

A close-up of the work to construct the GWR & GCR Joint Line near Wembley, showing the mechanical equipment that Watkin was able to deploy on what was called 'the last main line'. The Met line was just over the hill in the background and the tower now known as 'Watkin's Folly', has been abandoned due to subsidence. (*Record Office of Leicestershire, Leicester & Rutland*)

Alas he became ill in 1894, and, failing to recover his accustomed vigour, his plans began to fall apart. This process was to some extent accelerated by his character where, obsessed with driving projects through to completion, he had usually made bitter enemies of a legion of those he saw as opponents to his schemes. Thus he became more vulnerable and survived just long enough to attend the opening of the MS&LR from Manchester, via the Met, to his grand new terminus at Marylebone. However, as his Channel Tunnel had now been halted by the Government for fear of an invasion from the Continent, his 'grand scheme' was in ruins and, perhaps symbolically, his triumphal tower at Wembley was beginning to subside into the Middlesex clay.

Using the Met tracks from Quainton Road to near Finchley Road, the GCR – formerly the MS&LR, was opened at the new Marylebone terminus on 9 March 1899 with appropriate pomp and ceremony. The special train was headed by a pristine 4-4-0 11 Class A No.861 designed by the enigmatic Harry Pollitt for the new services. (*Chiltern Railways*)

WATKIN'S LONG SHADOW

As Watkin's health deteriorated, so did control over his empire. This period had a profound effect on the relations between the managers of the two railways that were to form his Manchester–London line: John Bell of the Met and William Pollitt of the MS&LR. A mutual antipathy had begun with their rivalry as junior clerks at the MS&LR, which grew as they were promoted by Watkin, and which came ever closer to an outright confrontation as the MS&LR was extended south towards joining the Met at Quainton Road.

The conflict was driven by their realisation that only one of them could now become the manager of their railways, which were inevitably to be merged into one. So, when Watkin imposed on both men an arbitrary revenue-sharing arrangement for the new London Extension based on the route miles of each railway, relations between them were brought to an even lower ebb.

By 1898 Pollitt had become so frustrated with the situation that he entered negotiations with the GWR – the old enemy of the Met! – about joining with them in building a new line they were already considering which would provide a shorter route for the GWR from Birmingham to Paddington. This would also enable the GCR to bypass the Met into London. As Pollitt increased pressure in this way, Bell countered this ploy by proposing to extend his Met northwards to join the MS&LR at Moreton Pinkney, thus increasing his mileage and share of the revenues. When this failed he resorted to prevarication, extensive litigation over an earlier agreement between them and even physical interference with the opposite party's trains.

With Watkin's death soon after the opening of Marylebone and the GCR, however, all prospects of a merger with the Met faded. Indeed, Bell and Pollitt remained uncooperative over the shared operation of the line between Quainton Road and Canfield Place, where the line to Marylebone branched off from the Met line to Baker Street. Although GCR trains used this route, the basic problem was that the passage of higher-speed GCR expresses was incompatible with the large number of slower Met commuter trains, and this was compounded by the friction between the respective operating staffs.

It was only the retirement of the two protagonists around 1901, followed by a disastrous rail crash at Aylesbury in 1904, which highlighted the dangers inherent in the present relationship and forced their successors to recognise that they had to work together. In view of the work that was now progressing on the parallel joint GWR and GCR line, there was increasing pressure on the Met to reach an accommodation, for this would mean that the GCR would no longer need the Met. So negotiations resumed from 1904, and with arbitration under Lord Robertson led to revision of the earlier agreement of 1890 for sharing the disputed line as follows:

1 A Joint Committee of the Met and GCR to be formed to take complete responsibility for the line from Harrow (South) Junction to Quainton Road.
2 Additional lines for the GCR to be provided by the Met from Canfield Place to Harrow at a rent of £20,000 per annum.
3 The Met Extension, with the exception of the Uxbridge branch, to be leased to a new joint body for £44,000 per annum.
4 The GCR not to convey local traffic between Marylebone and Harrow. Overall Met receipts to be protected and GCR fares to be no less than those of the Met.
5 Capital requirements to be funded equally by both companies.

A rare early picture of West Hampstead in 1901 with No.967, one of Harry Pollitt's Class 13 7ft 9in single-wheelers built in 1900. Here it is thundering past with the lightly loaded down 5.40 p.m. Marylebone to Manchester express. (*David Jackson Coll*)

Above: Another scarce photo of the newly-built GCR locomotive shed at Neasden with another Pollitt engine, a Class 11A 4-4-0, carrying the new express headlight code. (*David Jackson Coll*)

Opposite: Due to the congestion caused by the Met commuter and GCR express trains sharing the approach tracks to Baker Street and Marylebone, the Met was forced to build extra lines and lease them to the GCR. This picture of the separate bridges at Shoot-up Hill in Cricklewood epitomises the friction between the railway companies. (*C.A.F. Coll*)

A further example of Pollitt's Class 11A engines, No.857, hauling a down express for Manchester in 1901. Here seen approaching Harrow. (*Great Central Railway Society*)

Robinson built his Class 8F locomotives for the express goods and fish traffic, but in practice they tended to be used more on passenger work. This photo shows No.1099 heading an up train passing Wembley for Marylebone around 1910. (*Real Photographs*)

The final days of the GCR in 1922, with the first of the powerful Robinson 9P class 4 cylinder 4-6-0s *Lord Faringdon* thundering past Neasden with a Manchester express. (*A. L. P. Reavil*)

Under the Joint Agreement of 1906 the GCR, albeit with caveats on revenue sharing, were able to run a number of their local trains over the Met lines. This picture shows Chesham with such a train for Marylebone headed by a GCR Class K 4-4-2T. Interestingly, some of these engines were to return during the Second World War to operate the Chesham Shuttle. (*Ray East*)

The GCR also started to share with the Met the little-used local service to beyond Aylesbury. At one time the shuttle to Verney Junction was operated by a Sacré 2-4-0T Class 12A No.441 with an auto coach, here passing the goods shed at the northern end of Aylesbury Station. (*K. Nunn/LCGB*)

Above: The GCR sent most of its goods traffic via the GW&GC Joint Line, but here is one leaving the GCR tracks to run over the Joint Line with the Met. One of Robinson's ubiquitous Class J11 0-6-0 engines (called 'Pom-Poms' from the exhaust sound) heads a goods into Quainton Road, with the Met lines to Verney Junction in the background. (*John Gerchen Coll*)

Below: On the night of 23 December 1904, a GCR down express approached the Aylesbury junction at excessive speed. It crashed into the station and was hit by an up GCR train. Luckily there were few passengers aboard, but the crew were killed. Undoubtedly the acrimony between the Met and the GCR contributed to the disaster and this event led to the formation of the Met & GCJ. (*Rodney Sedgewick*)

Being Christmas, the train had a consignment of Christmas puddings on board and these were scattered across the station. Unsurprisingly, all of these had disappeared by the morning! After the crash No. 1040, a 4-4-0 Robinson Class 11B, was in a bad condition, but was removed to Gorton Works for repair and returned to service. (*Rodney Sedgewick*)

A view of the rebuilt approach to Aylesbury, looking towards London when the Met, GCR and GWR shared the station. In the distance the original GWR branch line from Princes Risborough is curving in from the right and the later Met line to London on the left joins it via a reverse bend, to use the same platforms. (*S. & G. Payne*)

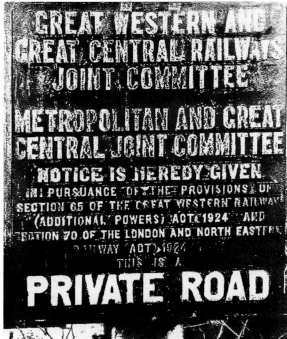

With the creation of the GW&GC Joint Line and then the Met & GC Joint Line, which both ran through Aylesbury, in effect it came under tripartite ownership. It was a complex management arrangement in which the overall responsibility for the station rotated between the three every three to five years and with the others taking turns to control the finances. This led to endless squabbles over major issues, such as rebuilding the station and track layout after the 1904 crash. Pity the poor station master! (*C.A.F. Coll*)

This came into force in 1906, however, although they 'buried the hatchet' they also 'marked the spot', both insisting on a rigid interpretation of a fifty-fifty share of traffic, costs, profits and support activities. Not trusting each other, this was enshrined in a side statement which closely specified the operation of the agreement, alternating every three to five years the relevant responsibilities for management, purchasing, shunting engines, uniforms, etc. Other activities were equally divided on an ad hoc basis, for example parcels were initially sent to London on alternate days via the Met and then the GCR! Maintenance of the track was divided at the 28.5-mile post near Great Missenden, where the GCR became responsible on to Quainton Road.

This Met & GC Joint 'Committee' filed conventional financial accounts and statistics. It comprised an equal number of senior officers from each company, as did the sub-committee of operating officers. At first they directly employed the staffs of about 181 (rising to 396 by 1947) who were responsible for most of the operations of the line. Initially equal numbers were transferred from the 'partners', and subsequently vacancies were filled in the same manner.

At Aylesbury the main GWR traffic was the service to Princes Risborough, with a few through trains to Paddington. This picture of 1930, looking north, shows such a train with a clerestory coach hauled by a GWR County Class Tank No.2222. In the background is the locomotive shed, which again was shared between the three companies. (*H.C. Casserley*)

A later view of GWR operations at Aylesbury. The platforms in the foreground were usually used by the GWR, but on this occasion, their auto-coach with 0-4-2 tank engine bound for Princes Risborough, are in the Met & GCR platform. (*C.A.F. Coll*)

Even the quietest corners of the Met Extension came under the jurisdiction of the Joint Committee. Here at Brill Station, the erstwhile terminus of the variously Wotton Tramway, Brill Tramway and the Oxford & Aylesbury Tramroad, the notice boards reflect the new operators. The Met poster optimistically advertises the attractions of London shopping. (*Ken Benest Coll*)

They had 'joint' uniforms, badges and conditions, but in practice some staff still felt old allegiances that could be revealed in making decisions – particularly signalling ones – which would favour their original company. Unfortunately the unresolved problem remained that the two companies had different objectives and, with an argument over even the need for replacing just one fence post, it is not surprising that the GCR (and later the London & North Eastern Railway) were reluctant to share the cost of the Met's capital investment for enhancing their suburban services.

In complete contrast, the GW&GC Joint Committee was willingly formed in 1906 by the two companies, united in the common purpose of the need for a new line that would give them mutual benefit. For the GWR it would provide a shorter, faster route to Birmingham, and for the GCR it would reduce its dependency on using the Met to get to Marylebone. Apart from the Met's failure to co-operate, their route took a steeply graded path over the Chilterns, involving severe speed restrictions at Rickmansworth and Aylesbury and which meant interlacing fast expresses with the slower goods trains and Met commuter traffic over just two tracks. Indeed, the GW&GC Joint Line was built with gentler gradients and curves plus adequate passing loops.

So, the GCR ended up with two routes into Marylebone, using the Met line for only about a third of its passenger traffic, but also for many relief, excursion and other specials. Against this background, the relationship between the GWR and the GCR was naturally far more harmonious, without the continual quibbling between the Met and GCR that continued through the subsequent manifestations of their Joint Committee.

CHAPTER THREE

SELBIE CREATES
METRO-LAND

BACK TO BASICS

The old order changed when Robert Selbie joined the Met in 1904 and became General Manager in 1908, particularly as his counterpart at the GCR was now the newly appointed Sir Sam Fay. Whilst they were completely different in character, with Fay being more extrovert and Selbie conservative, they both inherited the same basic problem from Watkin; he had bequeathed them both London Extension lines through lightly populated country, generating few passengers. Equally, they both carried the millstones of the large capital expenditures to build or upgrade their parts of his new mainline from Manchester to London. The GCR even had to buy its new rolling stock for the London Extension on hire purchase.

Whilst they were both faced with a similar problem, it must be remembered that the nature and scale of the two railways was completely different. The Met was a small railway, essentially serving passengers in central London, with pretensions to be a main line, whereas the GCR was very roughly eight times larger, reliant on coal and freight traffic in the Midlands, but with aspirations to be a national passenger line. Now that the GCR had an alternative route into Marylebone, the Met was of minor concern, useful as an alternative route, but supporting the Met's ambitions to expand its commuter traffic via the Joint Committee could be a potential drain on the GCR's limited finances.

Fortunately Fay had the foundation of an extensive strategic network, based in the Midlands and extending north to Blackpool and the east coast ports, as well as the new line to London. This was complemented by a Chief Locomotive Engineer, John Robinson, who provided excellent rolling stock: graceful locomotives equal to the best, comfortable smooth-riding coaches and restaurant cars, and wagons matched to the predominant coal and fish traffic.

To exploit this Fay showed considerable acumen by developing the GCR's commercial side to gain additional freight traffic to the south via London, and similarly passenger trains to places like Bournemouth, Blackpool, North Wales and even a through train from Aberdeen to Penzance. Indeed, another feature were specials such as excursions and boat trains to the Continent (albeit by travelling in the 'wrong' direction from London, eventually to Immingham and then by a GCR steamer). Gradually the fortunes of the GCR began to improve.

Met No.27, an Class A tank built in 1867. After spending its first twenty years working underground, now ending its life on the Extension fitted with a cab to protect the crew. Here seen trundling along with an up ballast train after passing through Harrow-on-the-Hill and bound for Neasden. (*Geoff Gamble*)

After problems due to the differences between Watkin and Forbes, the Met opened their branch from Harrow to Uxbridge on 30 June 1904. Due to the late delivery of equipment, electrification was also delayed and the stalwart Class A tanks engines operated the service. Here, the new station is in the foreground, with the goods yard behind. (*Unknown*)

Known as 'Pneumonia Junction', the primitive Rayners Lane Station in the early 1920s, with timber platforms and a small ticket hut on the over bridge. Beyond, the Met line to Harrow curves to the left, whilst the former MDR diverges to the right. With the rapid growth of *Metro-land* the station underwent several transformations to emerge as a classic Holden/Pick design for LT. (*Unknown*)

The first Metropolitan electric trains operated over the Inner Circle to alleviate the smoke problems. Inevitably they tended to follow the established American designs with open-platform entry at each end of the coaches. This shows a City-bound train of the subsequent 1905 design, fitted with sliding doors, at Baker Street. (*John Gerchen Coll*)

Harrow was now the changeover point between steam and electric traction. With Station Road in the background, two of the 'camel-backs' just off trains from London have been moved to the siding adjacent to the coaling platform. There an E Class tank engine waits to take over a train for the journey northwards. (*John Gerchen Coll*)

The first steps the Met made to electrify the Extension were to Harrow and with the introduction of electric locomotives from Westinghouse in 1905. This view from the bridge over Wembley Park Station, before the changes for the 1924–5 Wembley Exhibition, shows the 'camel-back' design with a central cab. (*C.A.F. Coll*)

The land Watkin had bought for his 'folly' at Wembley was later used as the site for the very successful Wembley British Empire Exhibition of 1924–5, which proved to be very profitable for the Met. With the Exhibition as a backdrop, this shows the scene looking towards Baker Street, with a variety of electric stock in both the new bay for the Exhibition trains and alongside forming City train. To the right is the Exhibition Amusement Park. (The New Zealand Railway Magazine)

Above: Selbie introduced the first of his new locomotives in 1915. Nominally designed by Neasden and built by Yorkshire Engine Co. the Class G 0-6-4T was intended to handle the goods traffic more economically than the earlier engines. No.95 appropriately named *Robert H. Selbie* after the General Manager of the Met is on an up freight near Amersham. (*J. Parnham*)

Below: The North end of Rickmansworth Station, in the early 1930s. At the start of the stiff climb over the Chilterns, H Class No.104 heads a train of Dreadnought coaches for Aylesbury. These engines were introduced in 1920-1 for fast passenger work and with their 4-4-4T wheel arrangement could also cope with the bends on the Chesham branch. (*J. Parnham*)

To cope with the increasing freight demands, the Met bought some First World War surplus parts for Mogul locomotives and in 1925, got Armstrong Whitworth to convert these kits into the powerful tank engines of the new K Class. Making a fine sight in 1929, at Aylesbury with a Private Owner coal wagon, is No.113 in the platform taking water. (*R.P. Hendry*)

By contrast Selbie had inherited a busy inner London line, but competing buses and trams were increasingly making it barely profitable. In addition, although Watkin's Extension to Quainton and Verney Junction had brought some of the benefits of modern life to sparsely populated Bucks (ranging from the telegraph with 'standard' Greenwich Time, to cheap fresh fish which stimulated the spread of fish and chips as a popular meal), it did not generate many passengers! Unfortunately, the favourable impression of the new GCR trains on Met passengers also showed Selbie that not only did he have to attract more passengers, but first he had to provide a much better quality of service.

As far as the Met trains themselves were concerned most still consisted of original open-cab Class A tank engines still hauling the old four- and eight-wheel 'bone-shakers', but now in the open and over the testing Chiltern Hills some 500ft high. As a result, due to the exposed nature of the route it was sometimes necessary to fit the engines with snow ploughs. Nevertheless, in the 1890s, they had bought some new locomotives: the disappointing Class D 2-4-0Ts for use on the ex-A&BR; the Class C and the Class E 0-4-4Ts to a design of Watkin's SER which were a great success and led to the Class F 0-6-2Ts.

By now the Met works at Neasden had gained limited constructional ability and made some of the Class E engines. Equally, better coaches with proper bogies had been obtained from Ashbury's, but this rolling stock was still inferior to that provided by the GCR and others. However, in one aspect the prospects were brighter, for Watkin had started experiments in the field of electric traction as part of his battles with James Staats Forbes over the Inner Circle. That this could avoid the smoke pollution encouraged Selbie to visit the USA in order to study their suburban electrification. This led the Met to adopt this form of traction and by 1907 their tracks were electrified to Harrow and thence the new branch to Uxbridge.

Over the following years from this base Selbie steadily improved his trains to become comparable with the standards set by the GCR, and extended electrification where it was justified. One of the reasons the Met became highly regarded was that he did all this methodically, economically and with a sense of style. On the steam locomotive front a range of new tank engines was introduced: the Class G 0-6-4s to cope with the growing freight traffic, the 4-4-4 Hs for the faster passenger trains and the elegant, powerful K Class 2-6-4s. These were complemented by some impressive new coaches whose spaciousness and smooth riding earned them the sobriquet of 'dreadnoughts' after the massive Edwardian battleships.

Here lined up for the 1933 Cup Final day. A posed view of the final type of Met multiple electric compartment coaches, designated T stock and introduced from 1925 to 1933 to operate the new services to Watford and Rickmansworth. With good acceleration and 'Dreadnought-like' comfort, they formed the mainstay of the commuter service. (*Getty Images*)

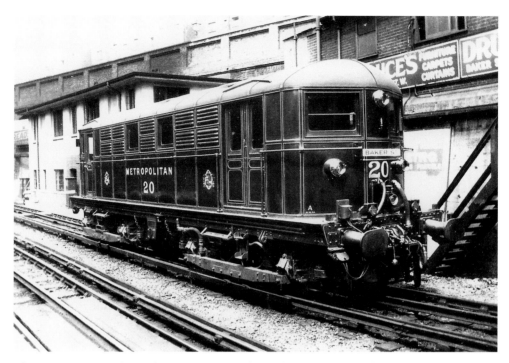

These iconic Bo–Bo electric locomotives were obtained in 1924, in time for one to be shown at the British Empire Exhibition. Four years later, No.20 in its original livery is seen here in front of Baker Street signal box about to return with a train to Rickmansworth. It would soon be fitted with a bronze nameplate: *Sir Christopher Wren*. (*R.P. Hendry*)

Electric stock evolved from the early American style open-ended coaches, via sliding-door stock, to the classic type 'T' stock slam-door compartment coaches offering high density – but comfortable – seating, and the acceleration needed on the Inner Circle. As electrification spread electric locomotives were introduced to haul the longer distance trains. Following experience with some Westinghouse camel-back designs and British-Thomson Houston Bo-Bos, the emblematic Metropolitan-Vickers Bo-Bo electrics were to be used for publicity purposes to epitomise the modern Met. They were stalwart performers for over forty years, showing a turn of speed and acceleration that equalled the best steam traction performance.

It was also Selbie's attention to all details of the Met infrastructure and operation that created an *esprit* amongst his staff and established a railway capable of attracting customers. Probably, the best example of this achievement in action was the changeover between steam and electric traction at Rickmansworth, in which the locomotives and staff moved with almost ballet-like precision to affect the switch in under three minutes. Although this improvement in the Met services was needed, its crucial contribution was to create extra potential passengers and freight to make it more profitable.

Left: As part of Selbie's campaign to equal the services offered by the Great Central over the Joint, and also get recognition as a mainline railway, he introduced two Pullman cars in 1910. They were called *Mayflower* and *Galatea* after famous racing yachts. Used on the longer distance fast trains, they mainly catered for morning and evening business travellers as well as theatre goers, who could enjoy a G&T for 6d! They were withdrawn at the onset of the Second World War and although afterwards LT considered reintroduction, the idea was rejected. (*LTM*)

Opposite: Visible by its flat sides, the third coach is the Pullman car on a down train for Aylesbury nearing Wendover. The locomotive is No.1 a Met Class E 0-4-4T, years later to be saved from being scrapped and now preserved. (*Lens of Sutton, J. Smith*)

TO *METRO-LAND, METRO-LAND!*

In contrast to the teeming Inner Circle, London virtually petered out on the Met Extension line before Finchley Road. The then population of the significant places that the railway was planned to pass through was not encouraging; for instance Harrow (12,000), Rickmansworth (5,500), Chesham (a surprising 6,500 due to local industries), Aylesbury (8,900) and Verney Junction (negligible!). Indeed, when the Met finally reached Rickmansworth typically only twenty tickets were sold each day! These numbers were most unlikely to sustain the Met unless there was considerable development to create commuters.

In retrospect, whilst Watkin's grandiose schemes seemed doomed his successors ben-efited from another example of the 'Law of Unintended Consequences' to an extent he had not envisaged. Watkin had acquired large tracts of land, not only to allow for more tracks and facilities, but also to ease his manoeuvres to outwit competitors. Also, in many cases the landowners, realising their bargaining position, would only sell large parcels of their estates. Another of his actions that subsequently made this land particularly valuable was that during the construction of the Inner Circle Watkin had to pay for the demoli-tion of a large City building, involving considerable expense. To defray this cost he was able to get a series of Acts through Parliament in the 1870s and 80s which uniquely enti-tled the Met to redevelop the surplus land for any purpose.

He first exercised this valuable concession to build a small estate for the workers at his new locomotive works in the countryside at Neasden in 1881. Sensing that this com-bination of having land and the legal right to develop it could be profitable, he built two further small estates for sale at Willesden (1892) and Neasden (1897). From his early accounting experiences with the Met he ensured that these activities were kept separate, under a Surplus Lands Committee.

Selbie realised that this experiment might hold the key to his need for passengers and in 1910 he embarked on a major thrust over the next twenty years to develop their surplus lands alongside the Met for housing. These estates would have to be near to the station, offering people the ease of commuting to London for work or leisure, yet also a return to their own place set in a tamed semi-rural environment. This was carefully arranged so that the Met would lead the developments by example, erecting quality show houses of varied designs (by the Met's own architect) at each site, and then selling houses from the Met site showroom, to be built by selected contractors.

Above: The Met increased the capacity of most sidings to accommodate at least forty wagons in order to operate longer goods trains. Here is one of the magnificent Class K 2-6-4Ts No.113 hauling an up goods near Aylesbury in the early 1930s. Interestingly, the train includes a presumably defective Dreadnought coach being returned to Neasden. (*R.S. Carpenter*)

Above: With the opening of the Met branch to Uxbridge in 1905, housing development started adjacent to the line. As this accelerated with the *Metro-land* campaign, some five wooden halts were opened along the branch. Here West Harrow is seen in the early 1930s with a T-stock train in the station. Note the early Post Office type K1 telephone box. (*C.A.F. Coll*)

Below: The Chesham branch had always been worked by an A Class tank engine with Jubilee coaches. But by the 1920s the locals had become very angry about the state of their trains. Eventually, the trains were replaced by E Class engines with Dreadnought coaches, although the locomotive still had to run round the train at the end of the trip. (*Lens of Sutton Association*)

Pragmatically, Wendover represented the limit to the development of *Metro-land* housing. But it generated extra revenue from serving the nearby Halton Camp based on a Rothschild estate. Large numbers of servicemen used the trains, and a branch was built to the camp to transport supplies. Note the Met & GCJ heading to the hoarding. (*C. A. F. Coll*)

In the 1930s at Chalfont & Latimer, a group of boys – reminiscent of *Just William* and his gang – reluctantly pose for a photo by a Bishop. In the background, an up Met train with a Class H engine and Dreadnought coaches is approaching past the Chesham branch train in its bay platform. Note the short platform awnings at that time. (*Bishop Rokeby*)

The Met profitably leased space in their stations for various kiosks and refreshment rooms. This buffet at Rickmansworth was very popular with both passengers and railway/bus staff. In particular, the three-minute changeover between steam and electric traction gave thirsty passengers the chance to enjoy a pre-arranged drink at the bar. (*LTM*)

Initially, London Transport continued the former Met's prestige Pullman Car service to remote Verney Junction. Here an elegant ex-Met Class H No.103 locomotive is being checked before departing for Baker Street – albeit with few passengers. (*Photomatic*)

Before: This is an early Met publicity picture of their first *Metro-land* Estate at Pinner in 1920. Two estates of largely detached houses, Cecil Park and the Grange, were built on either side of the line just south of the station. They were still set in unspoilt countryside. (*C.A.F. Coll*)

After: A recent aerial picture of the same scene. With Pinner Station in the centre and the Met line running diagonally from top left to bottom right. The previous picture was taken just below the railway line on the right and now the whole area has been almost completely developed. This reflects a growth in population from some 2,500 to about 46,000 in 1945. (*Copyright TGG*)

In this manner the Met retained overall standards and control, whilst minimising their own expenditure and risk. Not only did each estate contain houses of varying sizes and prices (within a certain range), but the estates themselves were aimed at different income groups. For example, the properties ranged from the more exclusive detached residences next to Moor Park Golf Course, to a mixture of detached and semi-detached houses in the Cedars Estate at Rickmansworth, to the more modest semis nearer London and beside the Uxbridge Line.

Inevitably, around these developments speculative builders undertook their own housing developments, illustrating how the plan gained momentum. Initially though there was a crucial uncertainty as to whether people would want to buy these houses outside London and whether they would be able to afford them. Fortunately this was a time of change, which created a very positive reaction to these options.

On the question of the desirability of living in a Met estate, the influential factors were: the wish of many workers to move away from the congestion and pollution of London to the advantages of 'fresh air' and 'a healthy life' and have one's own 'rose-covered home in the country'; improved communications and aspirations for wealth-creation and a better life; the endorsement of the 'Green Belt', giving a barrier to the spread of development; hope emerging after the First World War and the influenza pandemic, epitomised in Government promises of 'a land fit for heroes', 'in a green and pleasant land'; Ebenezer Howard's concept of the 'Garden City', followed by the creation of Letchworth in 1903 and others elsewhere, and finally the trend moving from renting to purchasing accommodation.

With regard to affordability, the influential factors were: firstly, the introduction of mortgages and hire purchase made the initial outlay seem more reasonable; then, as house-building volumes rose, techniques and purchasing power reduced house costs dramatically; lastly, following the depression the Government gave financial incentives to builders and in providing the complementary railway infrastructure.

Whilst these trends were naturally coming together, Selbie realised that the message had to be delivered to the very people he wanted to convince that the Met could provide the answer to their wishes. From this, the concept – or brand – of '*Metro-land*' was born, embracing affordable houses in a disciplined countryside with easy commuting to London. The term '*Metro-land*' itself was probably coined by John Wardle, the commercial manager, and was soon propagated by means of attractive posters, guide books, film and cheap travel offers linked to inspecting the Met estates. As the brand became accepted as the generic description of a lifestyle, it was adopted by authors, poets and composers so that it passed into common language as typifying a way of life.

As more moved into the Met estates and the publicity grew, it became a virtuous circle of success. Thus, by the end of the First World War these factors of aspiration and affordability had come together in a manner that made it apparent that Selbie had a major success on his hands, not only in generating passengers but also in transporting the materials to build the houses and the ongoing supplies. Indeed, the estate development had grown to the extent that in 1919 Selbie created an associated company for these activities, Metropolitan Railway Country Estates Ltd, to avoid possible criticisms of conflicts of interest.

CHAPTER FOUR

ALL CHANGE: FROM MET TO LONDON TRANSPORT

CHANGES OF OWNERSHIP

The magnificent effort of the Met and Joint Line during the First World War is described in more detail in Chapter Five, but the efficiency achieved was partly due to the establishment by the Government of an over-arching Railway Executive Committee directing all the many disparate railway companies across the country. Combined with the fragile financial state of most of the railways, there was widespread recognition of the need for rationalisation. Another factor that facilitated this trend was the important role of the Railway Clearing House (RCH), which was the 'glue' that had enabled the distinct companies to work together.

The ubiquitous RCH is now largely forgotten. It was established in 1842 out of necessity as the number of early railways grew, designed to make possible the complex inter-workings between them and to apportion costs and revenues. It was run by representatives of most of the numerous railway companies, and following 'grouping' in 1923, by the 'Big Four'. It eventually employed over a thousand staff and was later based mainly at Eversholt Street near Euston. Here all of the goods dockets and used passenger tickets were collected and collated in order to calculate the values to be apportioned to each company involved. This was then corrected on the basis of the relevant mileage, delays, losses, damage, demurrage and bad debts etc, with the resultant receipts being notified to the railway companies each month.

The RCH also kept an oversight of the inter-workings of the whole network, from producing its own working timetables and maps, to establishing standards for common equipment such as couplings, brakes and rolling stock dimensions. It also provided a non-confrontational forum for the companies to discuss policy issues.

Thus, after the First World War, both of the erstwhile Watkin railway companies came under new ownership. First, the 'grouping' of the mainline companies in 1923 meant that the GCR became part of the new London & North Eastern Railway (LNER), formed by the amalgamation of the lines to the east and north of Britain. A few railway companies, such as the Met and the Met & GCJ, were not included, but later this was to be followed by the Met being absorbed into London Transport (LT) in 1933.

These major realignments of Britain's rail system took place for various reasons. The 'grouping' of the UK's 178 different railway companies was an almost inevitable

In 1923 most of the plethora of railway companies in the country were 'grouped' by the Government into the 'Big Four'. The Met was excluded, but the GCR was merged into the LNER. However although the signage was quickly changed on the façade of Marylebone Station, passengers saw little change in their trains for several years. (*British Railways*)

Ex-GC Director *Jutland*, now renumbered by the LNER as Class D11 5504, heading an up midday train from Woodford over the Joint tracks near Chorleywood. This was probably a return working from the early morning milk train. (*John Parnham*)

consequence of the uneconomic multiplicity of railway companies generated by the enthusiasms of the nineteenth century, which overall were losing some £40 million per annum in the post-war period. Equally, the war had not only drained British financial and human resources, but it had dramatically changed forever the political and economic balance of the world too. Whilst, with the benefit of hindsight, these factors should have been recognised, in practice it was assumed that Britain's role would recover. In reality a short boom was later replaced by unemployment.

Against this background it had seemed reasonable to the post-war coalition Government of Lloyd George that the potential efficiencies revealed by wartime government control of all the railways via a Railway Executive could now be realised through rationalisation into four major groups. This was implemented by the Railways Act of 1921 and, in spite of various changes in Government, came into force in 1923. This created the GWR, Southern, London Midland & Scottish (LMS), and LNER as the main companies, although a number of smaller railways including two of Watkin's companies – the Cheshire Lines Committee and the Metropolitan – were not affected. Although the Met liked to claim its 'mainline' credentials, this exclusion from the grouping was probably due to it being embedded in the central London railway system, a factor that was to work against the independence of the Met some ten years later!

Within the new LNER, the GCR was grouped with the North Eastern, Great Eastern, Great Northern, Hull & Barnsley, North British and the Great North of Scotland railways, as well as some twenty-six of their subsidiary companies. The latter included the GCR share of the Met & GCJ so that, although the name of the Joint remained unchanged, the new LNER became the partner to the Met. Probably the GCR had welcomed the forced merger as their financial situation had been somewhat parlous, but it soon emerged that, if anything, the overall position of the LNER was still difficult and it was to struggle to pay dividends. This financial constraint was to make the LNER possibly even more reluctant than the GCR to fund its share of the capital requirements proposed by the Met to the Met & GCJ. In addition, the historical relationship between the Met and the GCR was now of even less consequence, as was the significance of the Met in the plans of the very much larger LNER.

Although Selbie had welcomed the Met's escape from grouping itself, the consequential more irksome relationship for the Met with the LNER in the Joint came at a difficult time for him, when he wished to embark on a number of major modernisation projects involving significant capital expenditure. These would require the LNER to acquiesce and contribute half of the sums involved. Of course the Met still had to finance the construction of all the necessary rolling stock to operate these track improvements.

The largest proposal was the building of the Watford branch, which had been delayed by the First World War. This also involved the electrification of the Extension from Harrow to Rickmansworth as well as the new line to Watford. In addition, at the Harrow North Junction with the Uxbridge Line the Met wanted to ease the congestion that would occur from the extra Watford trains by replacing the crossing on the level by a burrowing junction which avoided conflicting movements.

The GCR Atlantics, or *Jersey Lillies*, continued to work the expresses under the new LNER regime. Here No.5262 of LNER Class C4, having left Amersham with a down express, passes from the part of the track maintained by the Met onto that by the LNER. (*Unknown*)

In the years after the absorption of the GCR into the LNER their locomotives continued to dominate the London Extension. Here in 1931, a newly painted ex-GCR *Director* Class No.5505 *Ypres*, with an interesting variety of stock, nears Rickmansworth with an up slow from Leicester. (*R.S. Carpenter*)

Richard Hardy provided this picture with these comments: 'The train is the 4.55 p.m. Marylebone to Manchester, probably around 1937/8 and the location is about three quarters of a mile north of Chorleywood on the 1 in 105 climb to Amersham. The engine is No.6177 *Earl Haig* of the LNER Class B3'. (*GCRS*)

In the 1920s the dissatisfaction of the Chesham travellers reached a crescendo. Not only was there a lack of linking with the mainline trains, but they still travelled in the early rigid eight-wheel carriages hauled by the venerable A Class tank engines. At long last they were replaced by the more modern E Class locomotives and Dreadnought coaches. (*Photomatic*)

Above left: The LNER now partnered the Met in the Joint, and operated the Aylesbury–Verney Junction shuttle with a number of different engines, such as this Class F1 2-4-2T No. 5594. It is pictured here with its six-wheeled bogie auto coach at the isolated Verney Junction. (*Real Photos*)

Above right: A daily GWR milk train ran from Dorrington to Woodford Halse, where an LNER engine took it forward to the IMS processing depot at Marylebone. Above is the return train of 'empties' at Northwood and returning to Dorrington in the afternoon. The engine is ex-GCR, now LNER, Class C4 No.6085. (*C.R.L. Coles*)

The Met had long planned for a branch to Watford, but it was delayed by the First World War and then by the LNER replacing the GCR as partner in the Joint. They were reluctant to share the financing and even when work started in 1924 costly problems were encountered in crossing the River Gade. Here pile drivers are at work beside the river. (*Met*)

The LNER believed that the new Watford branch would mainly benefit the Met, but after much debate it reluctantly agreed to fund a 45 per cent share of the construction costs, which became even more when the contractor claimed increased outlay after encountering difficulties with the soft ground in crossing the River Gade. The LNER also insisted on being allowed to provide a train service from Watford to Marylebone, even matching the optimistically frequent service planned by the Met. Looking ahead, the LNER also claimed the right to be able to use its own electrically hauled stock over the Joint in the future. A strategic reason may also have been behind the eventual compliance of the LNER, in that access to Watford and possibly beyond would be a counter to the ambitions of the LMS to move southwards.

However, the LNER saw little reason to help the Met with its new junction at Harrow North. It had now inherited from the GCR the problems of their express trains being delayed by having to share the tracks from Harrow to Quainton Road with the numerous and slower Met trains. Thus, although this line was 'Joint', the junction was caused by the Uxbridge branch of the Met and therefore not the responsibility of the LNER! Eventually Selbie had to accept having to pay some 75 per cent of the £77,000 cost of the junction.

Whilst in the longer term the grouping of 1923 was to produce a complete upheaval of the railways in the UK, in the shorter term it seemed like 'business as usual' to the passengers and average railwayman. Although there were soon some moves towards new signs and liveries (for example the LNER briefly adopted 'L&NER' on their locomotives), the efforts of the new companies' Board members were directed more towards the jockeying between the constituent companies for the key positions in the new organisation. Inevitably, each of the companies forced to make up the new group felt that their own people should lead the new group departments.

The role of Chief Mechanical Engineer (CME) was typically contentious, with several large design and manufacturing works having substantial traditions vying to dominate the new companies. However, one rather different outcome which reflects on this story was that when the LNER came to select its new CME the position was offered to J.G. Robinson of the GCR. This was understandable on the basis of his seniority and record of excellent locomotive designs. However, Robinson, who was near retirement, magnanimously suggested that the younger Nigel Gresley of the Great Northern Railway should have the post.

As a consequence of consolidation, in most of the 'Big Four' a new raft of senior directors was appointed from the range of constituent companies. However, William Whitelaw, now the Chairman of the LNER, realising that 'rivalries do not slacken because a government passes an Act of Parliament', had a more relaxed attitude to uniting his group. He saw that there were some opportunities offered by the old GCR routes and their large freight traffic, and as these were exploited by the LNER there were no really major changes to the services from Marylebone over the Joint for some years.

True, the ex-GCR stock now carried the relevant LNER liveries, but W. Maclure (the doughty GCR Locomotive Running Superintendent) maintained his control, whilst at the level of operating officers for the London Division and Neasden Locomotive Depot, many GCR staff still continued in their posts. For example, Fred France who had been a fireman on the first train out of Marylebone was still on the same line, driving 'Improved Directors' in 1936!

Equally, because the Joint still continued in the new regime, all the stations from Harrow to Quainton Road still proudly bore their signs proclaiming ownership by the Met & GCJ. Whilst the LNER did not regard the Marylebone routes as of prime importance, they nevertheless provided competition with the LMS with the *Master Cutler* and *South Yorkshireman* expresses, as well as useful diversionary capacity for special trains, weekend excursions and goods trains to the west.

Such was the confidence in Robinson's engines that little use was made of those of other constituents of the LNER. However, by the 1930s Gresley's A1 Pacifics and his new B17 4-6-0s were briefly tried out on Marylebone trains and, with the latter finding particular favour, more of the *Footballers* followed in 1934. Then, with the increasing weight of trains, Gresley's successful A3s and V2s arrived in 1938.

As mentioned earlier, although the Met had avoided being 'grouped' into one of the 'Big Four', it was increasingly vulnerable to the pressure to unify all transport serving London. Although the Met and then the MDR sub-surface lines were the first 'commuter' type railways in central London, the world's first deep-level 'tube' railway, the City & South London, was opened in 1890 and was followed by a number of similar lines, largely backed by somewhat dubious American financiers. Their over-optimistic expectations were also tarnished by the rapid response of the omnibus and tram companies competing for the same passengers.

Against the background of deteriorating finances, the deep-level tubes began to acquire some of the bus operators and also sought to market their combined tube services through a loose association under the banner of the 'Underground'. This was to be expressed through the well-known red and blue roundel, to which Selbie quickly responded with a red and blue diamond-shaped logo for the Met!

An American, Albert Stanley of the London Electric Railways group, emerged as the energetic leader of the Underground 'combine', and, with its continuing financial problems, a formal merger was agreed in 1913 with Stanley as Managing Director. He was assisted by Frank Pick, who was instrumental in controlling costs and establishing an efficient operation, whilst Stanley was adept in persuading the Government that they needed to make substantial investment in transport for London, that just one integrated body was needed to deliver such a service and that his Underground was the ideal basis to achieve it!

The arguments of Stanley, soon to be Lord Ashfield, seemed to be in tune with the thrust of the mainline 'grouping' of 1923, and fell on the receptive ears of Herbert Morrison, Labour Minister for Transport. As Ashfield's influence grew in financial and political circles he obtained substantial Government funding for the Underground and this enabled him to get the Board of his 'combine' to agree to commit to Morrison's proposals for a London Passenger Transport Board. In spite of the following depression and the consequent changes in governments, the Act to implement the London Passenger Transport Board progressed on the momentum of the commitment of the Underground, and on the spectre of unemployment.

The Watford branch and the associated electrification were completed in 1925 and the service opened on 31 October with two special trains. One went to Watford from Baker Street with the Joint directors and the other, seen above behind Bo-Bo electric No.20, departed from Rickmansworth with local dignitaries. (*Met*)

Having successfully fought to keep out of the 'grouping' of 1923, Selbie now battled with equal determination to avoid merger with the Underground. To add insult to injury the 'Big Four' also saw advantages in a London Passenger Transport Board that included the Met, as this would mean that they had only one body to negotiate with in their complex relationships with the myriad of local railways in London. Equally, Selbie had few allies within London railways; even that old enemy – the MDR – which now peacefully collaborated in operating the Inner Circle, supported Ashfield's proposals.

Selbie forcibly argued that the Met was a 'different' railway to the Underground: longer journeys and Pullman cars, transporting goods, parcels and mails, integrating a high density inner service with a mainline operation and uniquely developing Metroland. He produced many statistics to justify these assertions, although in retrospect these were 'somewhat economical with the facts'. Nevertheless the fundamentals of what he argued were correct. Although he was well aware that the majority of those pushing for an LPTB would either disagree with or ignore his arguments, his strong belief in own position and an innate stubbornness kept him fighting for independence.

Indeed, he continued to put the rest of his efforts into improving the operations of the Met. The most important followed from the opening of the electrified branch to Watford in 1925 and the associated burrowing junction at Harrow, for this had transferred the problem of that congestion further south to the two track tunnel between Finchley Road and Baker Street. From 1921 Selbie investigated a number of options for 'bypassing' this bottleneck with new tunnels:

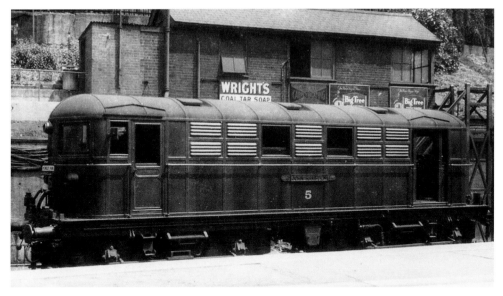

Later and less clean, another Bo-Bo electric locomotive No. 5 *John Hampden* is at Baker Street Station having brought an ex-Rickmansworth train into platform 1 and run back to wait in front of the old signal box, soon scheduled for rebuilding as part of the creation of a new headquarters over the tracks. (*Photomatic*)

After initial enthusiasm, the very frequent Watford services to Baker Street (electric) and Marylebone (steam) were poorly used, but the 1926 General Strike gave the LNER the excuse to cease their steam service. In later years, custom improved with the nearby housing development and here a typical T stock train waits in the station. (*H.F. Wheeler*)

1921: Finchley Road to King's Cross
1924: Finchley Road to King's Cross (via Primrose Hill)
1924: West Hampstead to Liverpool Street
1925: Kilburn to Edgware Road
1930: West Hampstead to Baker Street
1931: West Hampstead to Great Portland Street

Apart from the new safety objections to operating slam-door stock in tunnels, the expense involved remained a difficulty. It is interesting to note that the 1925 scheme got as far as new illuminated train indicator signs at Edgware Road incorporating destinations such as Verney Junction! Ironically, a further Selbie improvement of finishing the quadrupling of all Met tracks between Harrow South and Finchley Road, whilst benefiting the Joint services focused the Met's congestion troubles even more clearly on 'bypassing' the tunnel into Baker Street. With the other congestion problem of the irregular timing of LNER expresses delaying the high density Met services, Selbie made even less progress with the much more powerful LNER than with its former constituent, the GCR.

The Metropolitan Railway Development Act of 1929, which had facilitated the quadrupling just referred to, importantly also enabled the construction of a new Met branch line from Wembley Park to Stanmore. This had been under consideration for many years, including a link to their Watford branch for a *Metro-land* housing spread. Developers increased their pleas for such a line. However, both the LMS and the Underground raised objections, and this short branch was Selbie's answer to the criticisms of the latter.

So, in spite of the ominous threat hanging over it of being absorbed into the Underground, for the Met, 1930 saw much to look forward to. This included the completion of the emblematic magnificent new headquarters over Baker Street Station, with generous facilities including Chiltern Court containing some 200 exclusive flats (with up to ten rooms) and a 250-seat restaurant. Other projects included the extension to Stanmore and more plans to remove the congestion into Baker Street.

Against this background of his relentless drive to improve the Met, and a dogged battle to keep it out of the clutches of the LPTB, it came as a terrible blow when Selbie collapsed and died whilst attending a confirmation service which included his son at St Paul's Cathedral on 17 May 1932. It was very apparent that there was no realistic successor to Selbie, who at this crucial time combined such a detailed operational knowledge of the company with the ability to argue a strong case for the independence of the Met. This was confirmed by the Board having to appoint their chief legal advisor, John Anderson, as the new General Manager, and in doing so showing that he would be a 'caretaker', and by their recognition that the merger was inevitable – it was now a question of obtaining the best financial terms possible.

Although the Met continued with its strenuous objections, aided by some subsidies from Metropolitan Surplus Lands, only the volatile political situation occasionally raised hopes of a reprieve. Meanwhile the Chairman of the Met, Lord Aberconway, continued with negotiations to achieve an adequate settlement for his shareholders that reflected the value of their *Metro-land* investment. Eventually in June 1932 the Met Board accepted his proposals, in which he had secured valuable long-term guarantees of dividends backed by the 'Big Four' who were becoming increasingly anxious that the deal should be finalised. It was based on an exchange of Met for new LT shares, the existing debenture and preference classes for the similar LT 'A' and 'B' shares, whereas the ordinary shareholders were offered the option of either LT 'C' shares or a variant of lower value with a guaranteed dividend of 3.25 per cent for twenty-five years – which turned out to have been best option!

The 'associated' Metropolitan Surplus Lands Committee was excluded from the merger, the Metropolitan Railway Country Estates Ltd broke all ties in April 1933 and the Chiltern Court property became part of LT. It was perhaps symbolic of the spirit of the Met that, in the interregnum following the death of Selbie, the new branch to Stanmore was completed and opened on 9 December 1932. Bearing in mind the imminent end to the Met this was deliberately done in some style, involving a special train of new multiple-electric T stock, with, in addition, not only the Met Pullman car *Mayflower*, but also their Directors' saloon which had been rebuilt from the Rothschild's original private coaches! Of the leading managers of the Met who attended this valedictory event, few retained positions of seniority within the LT and all were phased out over the next few years.

Whilst enthusiasts and older commuters still remember Selbie's achievements with affection, today they continue to be shared with a much larger audience as a result of the works of John Betjeman. A particular feature of his centenary celebrations was his quintessential work in poems, books and films which encapsulated the pleasures – and the heartaches – of the Met and *Metro-land*. These works provide an ongoing memorial to those efforts of Selbie.

Above: The last defiant fling of the Met before it was absorbed by LT was the opening of the branch from Wembley Park to Stanmore at the end of 1932. Here, a few days later and now part of LT, a train of old Ashbury stock converted to electric traction waits at the platform alongside the Met 'diamond'-shaped station name board. (*Steamchest Publications*)

Opposite: Selbie built a fine new headquarters together with spacious prestige flats (together with accommodation for servants), a restaurant and a range of complementary facilities over the existing Met lines. Work on this complex site proved difficult due to the lack of space and desire to avoid interrupting the Met services, but to Selbie's immense satisfaction it was completed during his office. (*LTM*)

THE LEGACY OF *METRO-LAND*

In their publications, the Met regarded *Metro-land* as embracing all of their catchment area, though Metropolitan Railway Country Estates Ltd had created a core of some fifteen estates along the Met lines only for a distance which they thought corresponded to a reasonable commute at that time – namely to Uxbridge and Amersham. As these estates were successfully completed the momentum grew and other builders began to acquire land and develop estates adjacent to those of the Metropolitan Railways Country Estates Ltd. A number of these received 'official' recognition by being included in the annual issue of the Met bible, 'Metro-land', in which the attractions of country living and desirable housing were publicised in gushing prose and pictures. In parallel, speculative builders began to develop 'infill' sites and some local councils joined the London County Council in establishing low-cost estates in these areas.

All this construction work generated substantial increases in goods traffic for the Met but, more importantly, it also generated many more passengers who were to become loyal commuters on their trains. This was demonstrated by a fifteen-fold increase in workmen's tickets and a five-fold growth in season tickets, which meant that the Met achieved the best financial return on third-class tickets of any British railway, including the Southern. As a result the passenger revenues of the Met more than doubled between 1913 and 1939. In addition, the Met benefited from the handsome 8 per cent profits of Metropolitan Railway Country Estates Ltd which handled the *Metro-land* estates' activities. So, it could well be claimed that the Met, as well as *Metro-land* and its residents, had successfully achieved their objectives.

Undoubtedly it met Charles Pearson's hopes of a century earlier in helping those living in the capital to move into better homes in a more benign environment. The Met was the prime example in achieving this, but all the railways improved their suburban services, and the net result was that the population of London fell by about half a million, even during the surprising period of job growth there during the depression, whilst the suburbs grew by about two million.

Turning to the impact on the area surrounding the Met lines, which during Watkin's time had been referred to by his critics as a 'desert', this varied according to the distance from London. In that the development beside the lines was driven by the attractiveness of the housing and by costs, travelling a longer distance cost more in time and money but land prices were lower thus offering better housing. So initially the majority tended to move to housing relatively close to London. Equally, whilst Buckinghamshire did not have many substantial towns, they were sufficiently remote from London – and from each other – to be self-sufficient. Added to this was the attitude of the people, for whilst those closer to London were used to the concept of working there, for existing residents of a country village or town there were few attractions. Indeed, it took several generations plus the pressures of rising house prices to move the edge of *Metro-land* development out from Great Missenden to Aylesbury.

The influence of these various factors along the route of the Met is given below in relation to the growth of population, however it should be borne in mind when considering these figures that they may not be directly comparable in view of the vagaries of the censuses, boundaries and definitions. Nevertheless they do give some indication of the population trends, whilst the season ticket sales indicate the number of commuters (post 7.30 a.m.).

GROWTH IN POPULATION AND SEASON TICKET SALES THROUGH *METRO-LAND*

Location	Population				Season Ticket Sales £ in
	Pre-Railway	1921	1931	1939	1928
Willesden	100,000	165,700	185,000	190,000	n.a.
Wembley	4,000	18,200	65,700	121,000	24,900
Harrow	12,000	60,000	80,000	145,000	44,600
Ruislip	2,500	9,100	16,000	47,000	5,500
Uxbridge	8,000	20,600	31,900	45,100	5,000
Pinner	2,500	9,000	22,500	34,000	n.a.
Watford	40,000	48,200	58,500	70,000	2,600
Rickmansworth	5,500	7,400	16,000	47,700	7,600
Chorleywood	200	500	800	1,200	4,100
Chesham	6,500	8,000	8,800	10,000	5,000

Amersham	2,500	4,000	6,700	7,500	11,100
Wendover	2,000	3,000	3,500	4,500	890
Aylesbury	8,900	12,400	13,000	18,000	1,292
Quainton Rd	900	900	820	850	77

The size and rate of population growth along the Met reflects the date that the railway line opened at that place, the commuting cost and distance from London, and the availability of housing of various types. Whilst the season ticket sales are indicative they do not give the whole picture of the revenue from all tickets, with the demand for each type obviously varying with location. The lack of correlation between the size of the population and season ticket revenue for nominally similar places was probably due to the different nature of the residents.

On average the other tickets generated a similar amount as the season tickets, but there were some significant variations. For example, whilst (new) Amersham was an archetypal *Metro-land* town with season tickets accounting for more than 60 per cent of revenue, only some 4 miles away Chesham Urban District Council had sold its land for council housing, rather than to Metropolitan Railway Country Estates Ltd, and so they did not have a comparable presence. In addition, as a consequence of traditionally having a skilled workforce which now found better employment in London, there was a very large demand for workmen's tickets, for which Chesham Council had to lobby the Met during the 1920s. At the then limits of *Metro-land*, Wendover only produced 21 per cent from seasons and none were sold between Aylesbury and Quainton Road.

However, with the benefit of hindsight it is now possible to stand back and examine the broader issues of the consequences of creating *Metro-land*. Whilst the Met and the Metro-landers were largely satisfied with their decisions, many of the original residents of Middlesex and Buckinghamshire were unhappy with the developments, which seemed to have changed their traditional way of life.

Of more significance was the wholesale speculative expansion of the estates of the Metropolitan Railway Country Estates Co., followed by the usual retail outlets and necessary services. This continued unabated until the late 1930s when concerns about intensive development began to surface, restricting LT's ability to encourage such growth. After suspension of large-scale building during World War Two, however, speculative building began again, feeding on the pent-up demand. Soon most of the land along the Met out to Rickmansworth was covered by homes, together with that surrounding the stations to Aylesbury.

Nowadays, infill, together with the demolishing of the larger sites to make way for higher density housing, continues. Indeed, some would say that the very success of *Metro-land* has helped to destroy the essential character that once made it so attractive. But, whilst the older Metro-landers can point to a steady deterioration in their environment, the same is probably true of elsewhere so that most still find it a satisfactory place to live. Also some pockets still retain something of the rural character, often maintained by the growing nostalgic interest in heritage. Now, with a major expansion under way for Aylesbury, The Vale beyond might become the new *Metro-land*!

TO THE VICTOR, THE SPOILS

On 1 January 1933 the London Passenger Transport Board came into being, controlling most of London's public rail, tram and bus transport, and it was unsurprising that Lord Ashfield was appointed Chairman and chose his key administrator, Frank Pick, as the Chief Executive. It was a match of complementary talents which, by the time war intervened in 1939, had combined to create probably the best integrated transport system we have yet to see in London. In this an important factor was the creation of LT as a pseudo-public corporation, which gave it preferred status by having its borrowing guaranteed by the Government and thus stability to implement its plans.

Ashfield dealt with presenting the public face of LT and successfully cultivated the political and financial sectors, whose support was crucial to their plans for modernising and expanding the company. In this he forcefully argued that a comprehensive transport system for London was not only good for London but, delivered via LT, gave the most efficient and cost-effective way of achieving it.

In contrast, Frank Pick was less charismatic and lacked the ability to relate to his staff. However, his methodical, numerical and analytical abilities were outstanding in assessing situations and progressing solutions. In addition, he had a view that efficiently integrating the disparate elements that were to be LT gave the opportunity to do it in a manner that would positively benefit the passengers in a wider sense. This being not only with better travel, but by creating a coherent environment that would please, stimulate, and even educate. He believed that these benefits could be incorporated in the massive refurbishment and rebuilding he was undertaking, without undue extra costs.

In today's context such an altruistic mission might seem somewhat naive, but following the depression there was a groundswell to uplift everyone's aspirations. For example, at the same time and with similar motives (but with a strong moral purpose), J. Arthur Rank was spurred to establish a film empire ranging from production to cinemas. Nowadays such attitudes may seem overly superior.

Pick demonstrated a brilliant ability to see that all the facets of a passenger's experience on LT, from logos, to signage, design of rolling stock, buildings, uniforms, and tickets, could create an over-arching coherent whole to which the leading contemporary architects, designers, artists and even landscape gardeners could contribute. So, as the plans were developed he commissioned an eclectic range of rising contemporary artists and designers to produce and decorate the schemes.

These included Charles Holden, the architect of many of the new stations which are now recognised as classics, the distinctive lettering and clarity in signage as epitomised by the iconic railway map of Harry Beck and the outstanding series of posters by such artists as E. McKnight Kauffer. These works have come to typify design for this period and, bridging the divide between art and advertising, some even suggested that Pick's commissions were as significant as those of the Medicis to the extent that within LT his nickname became Lorenzo the Magnificent!

After the Met acquired the Duke of Buckingham's Brill Tramway, they replaced the rather decrepit stock they inherited with their own now venerable Class A tank and a Jubilee coach. Here in the first year of LT control, the peaceful scene with No.23 shunting at Wood Siding in remote Buckinghamshire seems unaltered. (*R.P. Hendry*)

The Met had enjoyed some seventy years of independent existence when it was taken over by the much larger LT in 1933. Frank Pick, the dynamic Managing Director of LT, immediately moved to rationalise and harmonise the Met into following LT practices. Here one of the LT inspectors (right), who has descended on Brill Station, is in for a shock. (*R.P. Hendry*)

With more options open to them, LT were able to solve the Met's congestion problems. As the tunnel into Baker Street represented a severe bottleneck, they diverted some of the traffic by extending their Bakerloo Line north in another tunnel through to Finchley Road Station to serve Stanmore. This 1938 scene shows the extra tracks being built. (*P. Hotchin*)

Nevertheless, before this aspect could really get under way his main task was to ration-alise London's disparate transport system with the objective of achieving better efficiency through uniformity and integration. In the case of the Met, Pick agreed that it was dif-ferent from the dominant Underground, but for the sake of the greater good of the new LT it would have to be made to conform to the standards of the majority and shed its mainline aspirations. Many in the Met did not like the inevitable changes and saw this as an emasculation which affected staff morale and worried passengers. However, although determined on the objectives of his upcoming review of the Met, Pick undertook it in his characteristic methodical and analytical manner, which involved personal study of operations followed by pithy memos signed in his characteristic green ink.

His examination of the Met accounts, combined with his instinct that all of LT's railways should be unified by electrification, pointed to the same fundamental questions over the future of the Met lines beyond Rickmansworth and particularly after Aylesbury. But Pick, who saw the significant financial advantages to LT of extending the *Metro-land* concept northwards beyond its current primary catchment area to Aylesbury, also realised that in view of the ongoing existence of the Met & GCJ the mainline beyond through Quainton Road was also sacrosanct.

So Pick commissioned a detailed study and visits to the anachronistic Brill branch and the line to Verney Junction. Both were memorials to Watkin's vaunting ambition, being respectively a line to Oxford and the 'Crewe' of Buckinghamshire. The financial analysis showed losses with little chance for improvement, so the Brill line lease from the descend-ants of the Duke of Buckingham was terminated and the Brill branch was closed on

30 November 1935. The line to Verney Junction, however, having some value for freight and diversionary traffic, was just closed to passengers on 4 July 1936 and later singled.

Subsequently Pick's hopes of emulating Selbie's financial success with *Metro-land* via the Metropolitan Surplus Lands and the Metropolitan Railway Country Estates Ltd were quashed. For by the mid-1930s the tide was also beginning to turn against indiscriminate suburban development, and Pick's proposals to apply the Met's development concession to all of the outer London area served by LT were firmly rebuffed by the Government. Nevertheless, he still saw the basic advantages in the extra rail traffic that could be generated by encouraging others to continue to develop housing commercially along the Met and the other surface routes. Thus LT went on advertising the advantages of *Metro-land*, although that brand name was gradually dropped!

However, as with other parts of the outer LT lines, Pick still felt that steam-hauled services were incompatible both with a modern system and with his desire to concentrate on electrification. As these trains were run in conjunction with the Met & GCJ, on which the LNER had replaced the GCR, he opened talks with their renowned General Manager, Sir Ralph Wedgwood. As might be expected this relationship was on a different basis than that between the Met and the GCR, because it now involved two relatively equal partners whose interests overlapped in other areas and thus there was more scope for negotiation.

In 1937 this led to the LNER taking over eighteen of the newer Met steam locomotives, plus freight wagons for the haulage of all Met-line trains beyond Rickmansworth. LT retained the remaining locomotives and wagons for works and maintenance purposes. The ex-LT locomotives were transferred to the nearby LNER engine shed at Neasden where they were gradually supplanted by ex-GCR tank engines, now LNER class A5 4-6-2 and class L1 2-6-4s. Most of the LT crews agreed to move with their engines, but only on the condition that they retained their Met employment conditions. The other drivers transferred to the 'juice' or electric stock.

Pick's personal observations of the Met at working level confirmed his suspicions that it had become increasingly over-manned, as labour costs in proportion to traffic income had risen from 49 per cent to 73 per cent from 1913 to 1932. He observed that many of the station staff seemed idle and that 'Spanish' customs were widely tolerated, for example non-stop trains tended to stop at other stations where it was known that a member of staff on that train wished to alight. Also train crews would sometimes swap trains travelling in opposite directions at convenient stations en route so that they got home rather earlier. Then there was the Chesham porter who retired to the top of the water tower to be out of sight whenever he wanted a quiet cigarette!

There were also pressures to adopt LT practices and standards on operating and engineering matters. Typically Neasden became subservient to Acton, but sometimes the idiosyncrasies of the Met defied the best efforts of 55 Broadway, the new LT headquarters. When new standards were promulgated for track clearances, the ex-Met platelayers duly slewed the rails through the sharp curve at Rickmansworth Station to their prescribed new positions – and stood well back to await events. The next LNER express took a ¼in off the edge of the platform!

With the extension of the Bakerloo line, new stations were built that made the equivalents on the Met Line redundant. Thus Marlborough Road Station shown here, and virtually unchanged from when it opened, was closed when the new St John's Wood (Bakerloo Line) Station opened in 1939. (*Unknown*)

A more recent view of the site of the demolished Marlborough Road Station. The position of the former footbridge can still be seen in the middle. The replacement of these intermediate stations eased the traffic flow through the tunnel considerably. (*Pendar Stillwood*)

Frank Pick of the LT inevitably wanted to replace the Met steam operations with a more modern form of traction, preferably to electrify his whole network. As a first step, an experiment was made with an AEC-built diesel powered railcar loaned from the GWR, here seen on trial over the Chesham branch line in March 1936. (*C.A.F. Coll*)

The next step by LT was to pass the responsibility for their Met steam operations to the LNER in 1937. Here in 1938, the former Met Class H 4-4-4T No.109, now reclassified as a Class H2 No.6421, is on a down train for Aylesbury passing Chorleywood Common. Sadly, subsequent modifications by the LNER spoilt their appearance. (*Locomotive Publishing. Co.*)

The Met Class G, H and K engines, with most of their crews, were transferred to Neasden LNER shed and LT just retained a few of the older locomotives for permanent way, breakdown crane and shunting duties. A former Met G Class No.95, now LNER Class M2 No.6155 approaches Moor Park with down goods in 1938. (*John Parnham*)

LT sold their engines to the LNER for £35,200 and then paid them 15s to 25s per hour for their work on LT trains. LNER No.6157 (ex-Met No.97 named *Brill,* after one of the smallest stations) is here on a passenger turn, about to return from Chesham with five Dreadnought coaches as a through train to Baker Street. (*Ray East*)

Whilst Pick maintained a constant drive to force the Met to comply with the general LT standards for railways, it was inevitable that the pace would be moderated somewhat by the previous traditions that were so deeply ingrained as well as by the somewhat laborious requirement to work through the Met & GCJ. But such was his nature that in parallel he also paid attention to the more fundamental problems of congestion that had so frustrated Selbie.

Indeed, now he had the flexibility of the much larger resources of LT in addition to the £40 million support that Lord Ashfield managed to cajole from the Government for a 'New Works Programme' – over five years – to improve the LT railway system and integrate it with the national railways. This scheme particularly involved the LNER routes shared with LT to the north of the Thames, of which the Met line was an important part. As the LNER saw that much of this work would benefit their own traffic it gave Pick extra leverage in his negotiations with them on easing congestion north of Harrow. Typically Pick then ordered a detailed analysis of the cause and effect of this incompatibility of their operations, with results that more than confirmed Selbie's instincts.

In practice the impact of the variable timekeeping of the longer distance LNER express trains over the Quainton Road–Harrow section was propagated across the whole of the Met network and Inner Circle, causing six times as much delay to the Met trains! Armed with this information, and the knowledge that the Government would support the necessary works, he was able to persuade the LNER to extend the previous agreement made to take over responsibility for all steam operations beyond Rickmansworth. Crucially the tracks north of Harrow into Rickmansworth would be quadrupled, all of which would be electrified as well as the existing lines to Amersham and Chesham. Interestingly, as a further step to reduce congestion, provision was made for a passing loop at Chorleywood.

The contracts for the major steel bridge works were placed with Fairfield's in 1936 and for the other civil engineering projects in 1938. In addition, Acton LT Works started the design of the multiple-electric stock to replace the T stock and Bo-Bo/Dreadnought stock that currently worked the Met Line. In the interim, it was proposed to convert the redundant Dreadnoughts into more T stock. As another indication that Met practices were not to be continued, the wooden mock-ups were all of 'open' layout, favouring standing passengers rather than the traditional compartments for *Metro-land* customers. Also, impatient to be rid of the anomalous steam traction, LT trialled over the Chesham branch in 1936 one of the new AEC diesel railcars supplied to the GWR. It was reasonably successful and Acton was commissioned to design a similar vehicle based on an AEC chassis, more suitable for the Met, but this was aborted with the approach of war.

The other serious congestion problem related to the bottleneck into Baker Street, and here the objectives of the New Works Programme for integration of the LT services with those of the main lines justified funding for a bold solution. Again Pick's options were now more extensive, and a ready answer was at hand in the shape of an existing proposal for extending the under-used Bakerloo tube line. By projecting the deep-level tube northwards under those of the sub-surface Met, emerging at Finchley Road to subsume

In the pre-war era the coal traffic to Neasden remained at a high level. Ex-Met Class K engine No.115 is handling the maximum load of forty wagons allowed over the Met, past the closed Waddesdon Station in 1939. LNER No.6162 Class L2, like the rest of the former Met engines, was transferred to another part of the LNER during the Second World War. (*Frank Goudie*)

Pick doubted the viability of the Met services beyond Aylesbury and ordered an inspection in July 1935. As a result the Brill branch was closed in November 1935 and the passenger services were withdrawn to Verney Junction in July 1936. Above, one of the last shuttles at Verney Junction, with the ex-GCR autocoach and ex-GER Class F7 2-4-2T. (*Richard Hardy*)

It took time for dominance of Robinson's locomotives to wane over the Joint, but gradually they were supplanted by the new designs of Nigel Gresley. However, in the 1930s they still headed most of the expresses, as with this LNER Class B7 No. 5465 ex-GCR Class 9Q on a train from Marylebone, passing Northwood in 1938. (*C.R.L. Coles*)

the role of the Met branch to Stanmore, it would take the stopping traffic and free up the Met. To realise this, the tracks and stations to Wembley Park had to be realigned and a further step to easing congestion was achieved by removing the conflicting access to the Stanmore branch by means of a new burrowing junction.

Parliamentary powers were obtained in 1935 together with authority for new stations and the necessary complex passenger interchange between the Met and Bakerloo at Baker Street. A consequence of the revised track layout between Dollis Hill and Wembley Park was that the old Met works and carriage sheds at Neasden were demolished in 1938, giving the necessary space for the new tracks. The depot was rebuilt in Holden LT style, even including an engine shed for the now much smaller number of former Met steam engines.

The effects of another piece of inherited operational complexity could now also be resolved. This had arisen from the prickly relations between the Met and the MDR over the running rights of the MDR trains to South Harrow, continuing onwards over the junction to the Uxbridge branch of the Met. Now with both parties subsumed within LT a reorganisation of lines eased the situation. Whilst the Met continued to use this route via Harrow to Uxbridge the District Line trains were replaced by those of the Piccadilly, merging with the Met at Rayners Lane and also running on to Uxbridge.

The importance of enhancing this capacity was due to the ongoing success of the *Metroland* campaign, with housing development along the branch generating an almost exponential growth in traffic in the 1930s. This meant that the revamping of the branch from, and including, Harrow on the Hill Station to Uxbridge, was soon incorporated into the New Works Programme. Rebuilding Harrow in particular involved extensive work, with excavation for a basement under the tracks to allow free movement of goods between platforms and access to the nearby main post office. It also housed space for LT staff sorting used tickets for forwarding to the RCH. Harrow was not completed until after the war but the resulting modernised stations, designed by Charles Holden and seemingly encapsulating the hopes of the late 1930s, are still regarded as some of his best work – work which would not have happened without Pick.

As the clouds of war gathered LT began to be involved with the Government as to how their resources could be deployed to support national security, and as to what preparations would be prudent, particularly against 'aerial bombardment' and for the production of armaments. Strategic reserves were created, buildings under construction diverted to the production of munitions and aircraft, unfinished deep-level tunnels allocated as shelters and secure control centres. An inevitable consequence was that the preparatory works for the quadrupling of the Met & GC Joint Lines north of Harrow were suspended and bridgework already delivered was 'mothballed'. Equally, some work on improving the Uxbridge branch was deferred until after the war.

However, in the case of the northern Bakerloo Extension the construction had progressed so rapidly that this was allowed to continue even after the war broke out, and the new line opened for traffic on 30 November 1940 as the bombing raids grew over

With the increasing loads of the Marylebone expresses, as Gresley's new Class B17, A3 & V2 engines appeared they were trialled. In particular, his Class B17 4-6-0s were very popular and so some of the *Footballer* batch began regular turns. This is No.2850 *Leeds United* with the 9.50 down to Manchester, near Northwood in 1938. (*John Parnham*)

LT built a new depot at Neasden, with a small shed for its remaining engines. They were now painted in a maroon livery with the London Transport insignia. In this new finish is L54, one of the Met's two Peckett 0-6-0 saddle tank engines which were used for shunting including the spells when the Met was responsible for Harrow sidings. (*R. P. Hendry*)

London. In consequence, as a wartime measure the intermediate Met stations between Baker Street and Finchley Road (Lords, Marlborough Road and Swiss Cottage) were closed in favour of the new Bakerloo Line equivalents, never to re-open.

In retrospect, the outbreak of war in 1939 represented a watershed in the development of LT, and certainly for Frank Pick personally. Having produced the plans for the evacuation of London and seen them work – with some 200,000 children being moved on 1 September alone – he was appointed to a senior position at the new Ministry of Information. However, he had a disagreement with Churchill over the use of what he regarded as dubious propaganda and was peremptorily dismissed. He died soon afterwards in 1941 from a cerebral haemorrhage. His memorial was to be a LT system that exuded confidence, consistency and excellence in everything from design to engineering, and with Lord Ashfield's help in providing the funding, this he delivered.

CHAPTER FIVE

BEHIND THE SCENES

For a small railway company the Met provided a surprising range of services. This was not only due to the nature of its catchment area and the growth of its interworking with adjacent railways, but also to the desire of Selbie to demonstrate the Met was of 'main line calibre' during its long fight for independence. Here are covered the efforts of the Met, in freight traffic and also in times of national emergency, illustrating its resourcefulness.

GOODS TRAFFIC

When the Met opened no service was provided for goods or parcels. However, contemporary illustrations show many passengers, particularly the artisans travelling third class, carrying some quite large items of their trade! Then, during 1866-9, Charles Pearson's original intentions of linking mainline railway termini came to fruition, with other railway companies' trains transiting the Met via junctions from the west at Paddington (GWR), King's Cross (Great Northern Railway and Midland Railway), Ludgate Hill (London, Chatham & Dover Railway), and the East London Railway to the east. Whilst passenger trains sporadically used these links over the years, it was the growth in goods traffic that meant that extra tracks had to be added to cope between King's Cross and Moorgate. Indeed, the main users built their own dedicated goods depots adjacent to these 'City Widened Lines' to serve central London.

The longest surviving example was *under* Smithfield Market, built by the GWR in 1869. It comprised a dense network of short sidings linked by turntables, over which the wagons were shunted by means of ropes and hydraulic-powered capstans to access the lifts to the market level above. Later vast quantities of meat were handled, initially from this country but increasingly from Australasia and Argentina via refrigerated ships and then GWR trains. At its peak, some 1.25 million consignments in a year were dealt with by over 600 staff. The GWR developed a series of their own tank engines, fitted with condensing apparatus, so that they could work over the Inner Circle. The last train to use Smithfield ran in 1960 and, apart from the occasional works or special train, the stirring sight, sound and smell of a steam train thundering through the confines of the Inner Circle was lost forever.

One market – that for fish at Billingsgate – did not have direct rail access, and each day hundreds of much-used boxes of fresh fish were manhandled through the nearby Mansion House Station on to the Met Circle Line trains. Inevitably there were constant complaints about the trails of malodorous liquid that covered the platforms and footbridge!

It was not until Watkin arrived in 1872 with his grandiose plan for a north–south railway, in which the goods traffic would be a crucial element, that the Met began to seriously develop its own goods service. In 1886 the first coal trains from the north accessed the Met via the new exchange sidings with the Midland Railway at Finchley Road. As Watkin gradually extended the Met to the north-west into Buckinghamshire, hopefully to join his MS&LR, basic goods and parcels facilities were provided at most stations by 1889. After some relatively unsuccessful trials with private carriers the Met itself started a door-to-door parcels service in 1893.

To further Watkin's dream the building of the link between the MS&LR and the Met began in 1892 and one of his favourite contractors, Joseph Firbank, was entrusted with the upgrading of the A&BR to mainline standards and contract No.7 for the construction of the tracks from the Met at Canfield Place towards the new terminus at Marylebone. The Met profitably transported all the materials and excavated soil, which amounted to some 1.5 million tons and was taken to be dumped at sites over London and in the gravel quarries at Rickmansworth for 1s per ton. As luck would have it, another valuable role for the Met was removing wagon loads of manure from the large number of horses that still provided most of London's transport. This was sold to grateful farmers in the Chilterns to nourish their thin chalk soil.

There are few records of the goods traffic over the completed Met line, but it is possible to infer from secondary sources the general level and type of goods carried by the Met at Aylesbury which give some qualitative indication of the activity along the Extension. From the opening of the line in 1894, the volume of goods dealt with quadrupled towards a plateau in 1904. By this time the incoming volume of freight had reached roughly four times that amount shipped out. Of the goods brought in, the largest category unsurprisingly was coal, followed by general items, then by minerals (building materials, etc.) and then by livestock.

The Met began freight services following the building of the Extension and with the completion of the exchange sidings with the Midland Railway, near Finchley Road in 1896. The traffic was mainly coal from the North and here A Class tank No.18 seems to have been involved in some vigorous shunting. (*M.F. Gates Coll*)

Soon, the Extension itself began to develop substantial goods traffic. In particular, Chesham with its many local industries became a major user. This scene of its busy goods yard with a standard Met Depot, a wide range of wagons and several horses, was photographed around 1930, in the last years of Met independence. (*David Steel*)

Similar levels of livestock were shipped out together with some general goods. So, it seems that at that time the general flow of traffic was inwards, mainly of coal and constructional materials.

As with so many aspects of the Met, the arrival of Selbie – wishing to emulate his GCR mainline competitor – resulted in an overhaul of their goods and parcels services. Firstly, as the Met still depended on borrowed GCR wagons, a fleet of some 465 Met wagons was acquired. In the following years yards were extended to be able to deal with a train with at least forty wagons, and the yard at Quainton Road was enlarged to become major interchange sidings with the GCR and others. For London the Met freight was handled at Willesden Green and the exchange sidings with the MR, who distributed the deliveries across London for them. Against this background, the Met decided that it would be more efficient to start their own distribution service with a City base for goods at Vine Street, adjacent to Farringdon Station, and a complementary parcels depot at Baker Street Station.

In his desire to match the GCR and other mainline operators Selbie introduced a complete range of goods services, from transporting just horses to complete hunting packs and from pigeon racing baskets to taking Bertram Mills' Circus to its winter head-quarters at Chalfont & Latimer. From the earliest days of the Met Extension they brought milk to London in churns, and soon dedicated vans for this traffic had to be provided. Later the churns were carried in the luggage compartment of the Dreadnoughts and required considerable manhandling from one platform to another. This continued until after the last war. The GCR also brought milk into London at a dedicated independent milk supplies depot near Marylebone Station. This was served by a special train of milk tankers which ran each day from Dorrington, and in the later years of the Met & GCJ it was usually hauled by Robinson's Director locomotives that had seen better days.

In the UK much goods traffic was originated and then delivered via the dedicated sidings of factories and depots, thus minimising trans-shipment. On the Met & GC Joint Line through Bucks there were a number of such sidings to serve the larger concerns. About half a mile beyond Aylesbury Station a coal concentration depot was established by G.W. Talbot & Sons for the National Coal Board in 1967. These busy sidings were manned by a succession of 0-4-0 and 0-6-0 diesel shunting locomotives until the depot closed in 1980. Another half a mile further northwards, International Alloy Ltd opened an aluminium recycling plant in 1931 next to the railway, served by a siding, later operated by its own diesel locomotive. After working to full capacity during the last war to produce high quality ingots for manufacturing aircraft, rail traffic ceased in 1968.

Watkin's expectation of tapping a significant amount of freight business at Chesham was justified, as shown by the number of goods office staff shown here and there would be others handling the collection and delivery. Ada Long, on the right, was the first woman to work there in 1915 and she later left to marry George Weedon, next to her, in 1925. (*Family of Ada Weedon*)

Left: Initially the Met relied on local carriers for distribution of goods at its stations. This early lorry was owned by the Catling family and is shown bringing baskets of the prized watercress grown beside the River Chess to Chesham Station, there to be sent to London and elsewhere. (*Ray East*)

Below: By 1919, Selbie realised that it would be more efficient for the Met to have its own distribution service. This was initially by horse-drawn vans and here at Vine Street (near Farringdon Station) is the depot serving the City. Although motor vans were introduced from 1921, later when the Met was acquired by LT in 1933, some forty-two vans with their fifty horses were still in service. (*Frank Goudie*)

Above: Transporting milk from local farms to dairies nearer London formed a steady business and, apart from stations, simple platforms made from sleepers were provided at various intermediate points, particularly on the Uxbridge branch. Initially the churns were carried in special vans, as above, but later in the luggage compartments of ordinary coaches. (*C.A.F. Coll*)

Below: George White was a parcels van driver at Amersham in the 1930s, here beside his 1928 Thornycroft which had been borrowed from the Watford branch – thus the sign 'Metro & LNERlys' on the side. He was well known for collecting 'luggage in advance' and on retirement kept in touch by running the bookstall on Chalfont & Latimer Station. (*R. Hardy*)

Above: Ernie Woodstock started with The Met & GC Joint Line in the goods yard at the age of fourteen years in 1927 and rose to be a senior station master. This picture shows him in the 1930s driving one of the ubiquitous Scammell three-wheel tractors. These were very basic and could be used with different trailers. This one belonged to the Met & LNER Joint Committee which operated the Watford branch. (*Phyllis Woodstock*)

Left: The Met was intended to link the mainline stations along the Euston Road and, although some passenger services ran, most of the traffic was of goods trains. When the Central Meat market was moved to Smithfield in 1868, the GWR joined the Met in building a rail depot beneath the Market, adjacent to the Inner Circle. This later picture shows the spiral entrance to the Depot adjacent to the Widened Lines. (*J.J. Smith*)

Right: One of the many trains of insulated meat vans serving Smithfield Market. Hauled by one of the GWR Class 9750 pannier tank engines fitted with condensing apparatus to work over the Inner Circle. The long load of *Mica* vans are leaving the Widened Lines, with the Hammersmith & City Station in the background past Paddington Goods Depot. (*Great Western Society*)

Below: A view inside the cramped GWR goods yard underneath Smithfield Market. The *Mica* insulated meat vans were often marshalled by shunting wagons on the 'fly', which required great skill by the driver in judging the speed of the wagon so it could be moved on the turntable whilst still in motion and yet end up in the right place next to a hydraulic lift. (*J.J. Smith*)

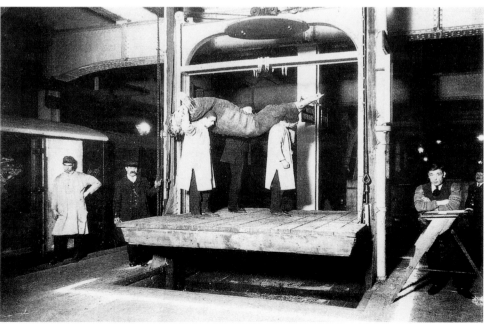

Even just before the parcel service ceased, this picture in December 1966 gives an indication of the volume of parcels once carried by the Met at Chesham. At that time they were handling some 65,000 items a year and here the Parcels Clerk, Bob Bignall, with two station men, are checking a nostalgic array of Christmas gifts. (*R. Bignall*)

Above: 'By dawn's early light', a green BR Class 115 DMU with yellow 'whiskers' has delivered the morning newspapers along the Met to Chesham in July 1962 and is now being prepared to form the unpublicised 05.58 a.m. to Marylebone, often used by early City workers. This service was the last reminder that this branch was once part of the Met & GCJ. (*G.H. Hunt/Colour-Rail LT191*)

Above: The coal concentration depot at Griffin Lane, near Aylesbury, was initially operated by G.W.Talbot and then by the NCB served by sidings from the main Met & GC Joint Line.The locomotive pictured was an ex-BR diesel mechanical 0-6-0 No.D2324.Traffic ceased by 1990. (*Bucks County Museum Photo Archive*)

Opposite below: By the late 1960s, the goods yard at Aylesbury was one of the few to survive as a concentration depot and had its own diesel shunters.This is the scene looking north from the station towards Quainton Road with two trains headed by BR Class 25 diesel locomotives. (*Ron Potter*)

Further along the line the Brill Tramway was originally built by the Duke of Buckingham to improve the performance of his estate, and in doing so to serve the various activities going on there, thus sidings were laid to a brick and tile works, gasworks and an agricultural machinery factory.When Baron Ferdinand de Rothschild decided to build his chateau on the hill at Waddesdon, a siding was laid from the Brill branch to take materials to the site and was used for many years.

Until the end of the Second World War the railways were the prime method of distributing the newspapers that then were mainly printed in Fleet Street. For years such a train left Marylebone at 2.30 a.m. with a heavy load and a timing that made it one of the most onerous schedules over the Met & GC Joint Line (less than forty-four minutes to Aylesbury was usually achieved). Another early morning newspaper train ran to Chesham, dropping off loads for the newsagents en route.This Marylebone service was maintained until 1962, latterly by a diesel multiple unit (DMU).

Initially the Met depended on Pickfords for the actual delivery service in London and local carriers for the Met & GC Joint stations along the Extension. In 1909, however, Selbie found that it would be cheaper to establish their own cartage services. Horse-drawn wagons were used at first, but by the early 1920s electric vehicles were trialled followed by various makes of motor vans.Although some horse-drawn wagons were still in use until the end of the Met, the pride of the fleet were the Thornycroft motor vans in their smart cream and brown livery carrying the latest *Metro-land* posters. Now with this service for parcels and goods Selbie could proudly offer his customers a reasonably competitive service to that of his mainline competitors.

As a result of these efforts, by the late 1920s the Met goods traffic rose to a value of some £110,000 per annum, roughly 30 per cent of that generated by passengers. Of this sum about 40 per cent arose from coal, 32 per cent from other minerals, 25 per cent from merchandise, 1 per cent from livestock and 2 per cent from miscellaneous categories.This traffic was fairly evenly spread over the Extension line, with the busier stations like Willesden Green, Harrow, Pinner, Rickmansworth, Chesham and Aylesbury each handling about 5,000 tons a year. However, in common with all other railways a decline began in the 1930s due to the rise in competition from road transport.

WARS, OUTRAGES & ACCIDENTS

We now appreciate the value of the railways to our nation's defence, but this was not always so. At the beginning of the railway age in the 1830s we tend to think of the objections to this new mode of transport as mainly coming from the landed gentry and the church estates, who were concerned about the potential disruption of their traditional way of life. Whilst to an extent this was true, in reality the main anxiety was from the Establishment, who were worried that the easier communication and mobility provided by the railways would encourage the radical elements amongst the working classes and lead to unrest and possible insurrection.

It must be remembered that the consequences of the French Revolution were still lingering, and the influential Duke of Wellington was amongst those in the army who held strong reservations about the social impact of the railways. In adopting this view he was probably influenced by events when he formally opened the first major railway between Liverpool and Manchester in 1830. For when his train arrived at Manchester he was met by a large and hostile crowd wearing the tricolour cockades supporting the French Revolution, leading him to comment that 'railways would simply encourage the lower classes to travel about'. Yet within a few years the army itself was using trains to transport troops to quell the Chartist riots.

Typically, the development of railways to the north-west of London, which was of particular interest to Watkin, was initially blocked on these grounds by the Grenville family who owned large tracts of Buckinghamshire – and also the local press! Their stance was reversed by the more forward-looking incoming Third Duke of Buckingham, who realised that railway access could actually help to save the impoverished estates that he had just inherited from the virtually bankrupt Second Duke. Indeed, he soon promoted a number of local railways, became Chairman of the LNWR and for a while he was actually an associate of Watkin. Indeed, by the time the inevitable financial bubble of the 'Railway Mania' burst, many landowners had become investors and were also willing to sell their land for railway development, at a price of course.

Whilst the railways did influence social aspirations, their impact was as part of the larger changes brought about by the Industrial Revolution. Although the reservations of the army remained, in 1855 they had to call on Watkin and Charles Liddell (his engineer) to advise on the logistics for the Crimean War and then build a railway from Balaclava using British navvies to assist in the capture of Sevastopol. The army also noted the use of railways in the American Civil War. By the 1880s railways were commonly being used to transport troops and equipment, so when Watkin commenced building his Channel Tunnel in 1881 the army now opposed it bitterly on the grounds that French troops could use it to invade Britain. In spite of Watkin's offer to install gates to flood the tunnel and a spiral approach to the French entrance (to give the British Navy the maximum chance of shelling the French troop trains!), the army influenced the Government to eventually close the workings.

Below: The Boer War was the first conflict to involve the transport of troops by rail in significant numbers. In many ways a typical picture, this scene shows a large crowd welcoming the return of troops from South Africa at Aylesbury Station in 1901. (*Bucks County Museum Archive*)

Above: From the outbreak of the First World War in 1914 there was an increasing demand for wooden structures needed for the Front in France. Trench boarding and posts came via Wendover Station from the nearby woods and this train at Chesham, headed by A Class tank No.48, is loaded with kits of huts for France. (*Ray East*)

Below: During the First World War, most of the Army transport was horse-drawn and this scene would have been typical of many Met stations at that time. In the Goods Yard at Rickmansworth, a number of army limber wagons of the Overseas Dominions Artillery Regiment are being prepared for loading on to flat trucks for moving to France. (*C.A.F. Coll*)

Above: Aerial warfare during the First World War brought home to the UK public the horrors of war for the first time. Here a bomb dropped by a Zeppelin airship hit the Met tracks near Moorgate on the Widened Lines and this shows the workmen repairing the damage to the track power supplies. (*LTM*)

Below: During the First World War, the War Department built a light railway to serve their camp at Halton. This was encouraged by the Met to join their mainline at Wendover Station. The base was expanded considerably during the Second World War. Seen here is a Fowler 0-4-0 diesel engine AMW No.119 hauling a train of coal trucks near the canal bridge on the branch. (*A.J. Reed*)

In order to sustain the war efforts British railways have relied on the large-scale employment of female workers. Seen here in 1916 during the First World War, a female Met guard is giving 'the away' to a multiple electric stock train on the Uxbridge branch. Note the milk churns on the platform from one of the many dairies still adjacent to the line as far as Wembley. (*Getty Images*)

Women porters are seen here in 1914 cleaning GCR carriages at Marylebone. Such cleaning by hand emphasises the massive dependence of industry on the relatively cheap manual labour. (*Getty Images*)

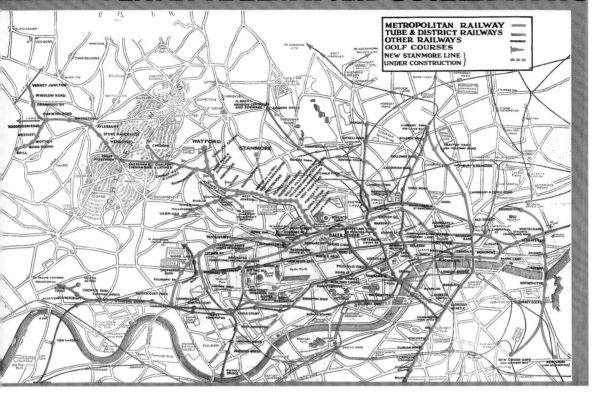

1. Showing the new branch to Stanmore then under construction, this was the last map issued by the Met, before being absorbed into LT in 1933. As usual it is distorted to emphasise the coverage of central London, whilst making *Metro-land* seem easily accessible. (*C.A.F. Coll*)

2. The Metropolitan Railway at King's Cross Station opened in 1863, with the aid of the Great Western Railway who had invested money to ensure that a third rail was added to enable their broad-gauge trains to access the city. This was fortunate, as the new Met 'smokeless' locomotives were a failure and they had to rely on those from the GWR. (*Unknown*)

3. Without their own engines, the Met quickly obtained some 4-4-0T from Beyer-Peacock intended for overseas. These proved most successful and became the mainstay of their services for many years. Later cabs were added to protect the crews during bad weather when above ground. (*C.A.F. Coll*)

4. The well-known railway artist, Peter Green, has recreated the sight of one of Robinson's largest GCR express passenger engines, *Lord Faringdon*, racing through Pinner Station with a train bound for Marylebone, around 1920. These class 9P 4-6-0 locomotives were heavy on coal but could give excellent performances. (*Peter Green*)

5. The Met displayed this striking large relief map at Baker Street Station for many years and it clearly shows the barrier formed by the Chiltern Hills which proved such a problem to the builders of the first railways to the northwest of London. It is also roughly to scale and therefore demonstrates how Watkin's ambitions greatly extended the Met from its short underground origins. (*LTM*)

6. *Below:* In 1938, Gresley's new locomotives were gradually taking over on the old GCR line, but many of Robinson's fine engines were still to be seen. Here, one of his C4 Class No. 5194 Atlantics, in good fettle and with an LMS leading coach, is leaving Aylesbury Station for Marylebone. With the outbreak of war the GC types remained the mainstay of the route. (*Pendragon Collection/Colour-Rail*)

Visit the Glorious Countryside
Served by the "Metro"
DAY and HALF DAY EXCURSIONS

SEE HANDBILLS FOR FULL PARTICULARS
OR OBTAIN INFORMATION DIRECT FROM
COMMERCIAL MANAGER, BAKER ST. STATION N.W.I.

BAKER ST STATION
N.W.I.

R. H. SELBIE
GENERAL MANAGER

7. The transformation by Selbie of the Met publicity is shown by the change from the Victorian style that he inherited in the early 1900s (*opposite*), to the modern, impressionistic approach of the 1930s (*left*), directed at boosting *Metro-Land*. (*C.A.F. Coll*)

8. *Below:* In 1958 a former GCR Locomotive Class 9K 4–4–2T (and now BR No.67416) comes to the crest of the 1 in 66 climb up the Chesham Branch near Raans Farm to Chalfont. These locomotives were soon to be replaced by a succession of ex–LMS and BR tank engines. (*S.M. Watkins/Colour-Rail*)

9. A close-up of a venerable Met Ashbury coach, the survivors of which ended their days on the Chesham Shuttle. Their appearance is characteristic of the Metropolitan Railway stock, being built around 1898 for steam haulage, then converted for electric traction and finally reverting for use with the Chesham Shuttle in 1940. (*C.A.F. Coll*)

10. August 1961 and the tracks have been quadrupled between Northwood and Moor Park in preparation for the electrification to Amersham and Chesham. However, whilst the new A60 stock is still awaited a trusty Met 6-car T stock train heads on the fast line into stormy weather. (*Stephenson Locomotive Society/Colour-Rail*)

11. Later in 1961 one of the pristine new A60 8-car trains is in Rickmansworth south sidings, whilst in the foreground veteran Met Bo-Bo electric Locomotive No.8 *Sherlock Holmes* heads an Aylesbury train of 'Dreadnoughts' for one of the last of the polished changeovers to steam traction at the station. (*J.B. Snell/Colour-Rail*)

12. With the end in sight for steam services from Marylebone, in 1965 a BR Class 7P Britannia Pacific *Byron*, only built in the 1950s but now ill-cared for, hauls a semi-fast to Nottingham near Wendover in the late afternoon sunlight. (*J.P. Mullett/Colour-Rail*)

13. A 2008 picture that encapsulates the ongoing revival of the services from Marylebone. Symbolically on the left of the scene is the new Wembley Stadium, whilst on the old GC link from the GW&GC Joint Line, one of the first Wrexham & Shropshire Railway trains headed by two Class 67 diesels heads to London. To the right is the new Chiltern Railways base with a Turbostar DMU. (*Brian Morrison*)

14. One of the new TfL S8 stock (sub-surface/eight-car) trains built by Bombardier to replace the ageing A60 stock on the Met line and due to enter service in 2010. The low slung body, to enable easy access of wheelchair users from platforms and the flexible connection between coaches, can be seen. (*C.A.F. Coll*)

On 11 November 1918 an Armistice was declared. As can be seen, this Met electric 1905-7 set on the Inner Circle carries a Union Flag in the cab to mark the event. Behind can be seen a Met train of Ashbury coaches, going in the opposite direction. (*LTM*)

Nevertheless, Britain itself now began to regularly use the railways to move servicemen, their equipment and supplies around the country. The first major campaign to employ our railways on a significant scale was the Boer War of 1899-1902. As with other railways, the Metropolitan Railway was involved with the transit of other companies' trains of three different types: troop trains, ambulance trains and numerous coal trains for refuelling the Royal Navy. Also by this time Britain was building railways in most parts of the Empire, such as Egypt and India, not only to improve communications but also to enable the rapid deployment of the army.

With the First World War of 1914-18, the scale and nature of the involvement of the Met and GC Railways radically increased. Not only were very large numbers of servicemen to be moved, but it also involved at least as many horses with their provender. Significantly, this was also the first time the war really had a direct impact on people in Britain: the sight of crowded troop trains departing for the Front and then the ambulance trains arriving back in London full of the wounded; the shortage of supplies due to U-boat warfare and the bombing of London by Zeppelins and then aircraft made the realities of modern warfare very apparent to the civilian population. By comparison with later wars, these aerial attacks were of a minor nature (though they badly affected morale) and the Met was hit by only one bomb, near Aldersgate, which cut the power supply to the tracks.

With the menace from German submarines to our coastal shipping, virtually all of the vast amount of coal that was now needed was transported by rail. Coal for the Royal Navy was a major demand (transported via so-called 'Jellicoe trains'), but probably the main contribution of the railways was the movement of munitions and materials for the

During the Blitz, London's City and Docks suffered the most damage. This picture was taken on 8 October 1941 and shows the result of the bombing on the previous night of the City Widened Lines at Moorgate. All of the office buildings and warehouses are burnt out, whilst in the foreground are the remains of an LTR stock train. (*LTM*)

army fighting in France. Inevitably the Met carried some of this transit traffic but also provided trains for the numerous camps in its catchment area and specific supplies.

An example of these activities was the wartime development of the estate of Anthony de Rothschild at Wendover. Initially the beech woods had been used to provide wood for building the trenches, and then the estate had been given over completely to the army which then gave way to the Royal Flying Corps. At the suggestion of the Met station-master, a military light railway to remove the wood and also supply provisions for the camp was built to join the Met. The local industries of the Chilterns supplied everything from boots to wooden huts for the army.

As Christian Wolmar has pointed out, the role of the railways was vital, with Watkin's Met playing a surprisingly significant part in the war. The system offered a route through London on the City Widened Lines, a link built in the 1860s allowing trains to reach the rail network south of the Thames. This was one of only four connections across the capital, and the most direct. Consequently it was used intensively by troop and other special trains, with an average of sixteen military trains every day throughout the conflict in addition to the normal Met services. At the peak, during one fortnight in the build-up to the offensive in 1915, there were an overwhelming 210 trains on those tracks daily, one every seven minutes around the clock.

Above: To the right of the previous picture of Moorgate, in January 1942, the buildings remain shells but the tracks are repaired. After a fall of snow, an LT train hauled by an ex-Met Class F 0-6-2T is carrying replacement lengths of rail. Behind are wagons of rubble. (*LTM*)

Left: On 11 September 1940 Marylebone was put out of action by high explosive and unexploded bombs, including one on the St John's Wood Tunnel; however, within a few days a temporary terminus of sleepers had been created at Neasden. This picture on 16 October shows a LNER train preparing to reverse, whilst a Bakerloo train arrives from Stanmore. (*London Railway Record*)

The scale of the effort of all the railways in this country is illustrated by the simple statistic that 2.68 million sick and wounded soldiers were carried on the railways during the war, with the Met handling some 26,000 special trains over the City Widened Lines. In this and many other ways the railways had performed well during the war, and the assumption was that they would be paid for their efforts. However, no settlement was made until well after the war, when the Treasury reluctantly paid for the contracted services, but at pre-war rates and excluding the many emergency activities they had performed. This started the steady decline in support for the railways by subsequent governments. Indeed, following events only compounded their financial problems, with the General Strike in 1926 and then the depression. Paradoxically, the large numbers of surplus army vehicles becoming available at low prices after the war had also encouraged a competitive motor transport industry.

At the outbreak of the war the crucial role of the railways, coupled with the shortage of manpower and essential materials, led to the creation of a Railway Executive to manage the many railway companies for the war effort. Senior Officers of the Met and GCR served in the Railway Executive, and to ease the shortage of staff both railways recruited numbers of women as guards, cleaners and ticket clerks. Although the Railway Executive ceased with the end of the war, the improvements in efficiency that it had achieved increased the political pressure for a rationalisation of the 120 different companies that then operated in Britain.

So, with the outbreak of the Second World War in 1939 a Railway Executive Committee (REC) was again quickly imposed to coordinate all the resources of the now 'Big Four' railways and LT to meet the escalation in the German threat epitomised by the Blitzkrieg and their indiscriminate use of new weapons. Initially under Pick's plans 500,000 children were evacuated from inner London in four days, with the Met & GCR running many specials to Buckinghamshire. Vital organisations were also moved, the RCH being relocated to Amersham.

An extra burden was the imposition of a rigid blackout to avoid attracting enemy aircraft, with the open cabs of the engines being covered with sheeting and miniscule lighting in the coaches. Apart from the numerous troop, gas decontamination and ambulance trains, huge amounts of materials and supplies were also moved by rail. To cope with the demand the REC took control of the entire fleet of 1.2 million railway and privately owned wagons, and by more efficient utilisation were able to carry 50 per cent more freight.

The Joint Line through Bucks served an area that became the location for many vital wartime activities: aerodromes at Northolt, Halton, Westcott and Bovingdon; camps in the Chilterns and vital industries such as International Alloys producing aluminium for aircraft. Virtually all the furniture manufacturers turned to war work, with wooden airframes for the Mosquito being typical items. The Met & GC Joint Line turned out to be useful not only for direct traffic but also for diverting it around London via the LMS Oxford & Cambridge line, with a new junction (Shepherds Furze Curve) to facilitate this being built at Calvert. Even the then little-used line to Verney Junction was pressed into service for specials, such as a train carrying the Russian Foreign Minister, Molotov, to a meeting with Churchill in May 1942. Due to shortages, old rolling stock was returned to traffic, with the original Victorian

Clearing up after Neasden LT sheds were bombed in October 1940 and in which the offices were demolished and the train sheds were badly damaged. This included some Bakerloo trains serving the Stanmore branch. (*LTM*)

Ashbury coaches being used to form the Chesham Shuttle hauled by venerable ex-GCR C13 tank engines. To make matters worse for the maintenance of the rolling stock, most railway workshops, such as LT Neasden, were turned over to produce armaments.

This time the railways were a prime objective of German bombers, and those in London suffered severely. Although little happened until the Germans had invaded France, the main aerial Blitz of Britain lasted from September 1940 until May 1941, and then continued at a lower level until the 'baby Blitz' of January to April 1944. Inevitably most of the bombing was concentrated on central London, the City and the docks, although other targets were hit in the Met area out to Uxbridge, Watford and Aylesbury, and bombers returning to their bases would unload their bombs anywhere.

In crude terms most bombs were dropped on the Met along the line from Neasden and particularly along the Inner Circle. In the latter context, the strategically important City Widened Lines and mainline stations (including Marylebone and Baker Street) were badly affected. In the first Blitz there were over thirty major disruptions to the Met due to bombing, ranging from incendiaries and high explosives to aerial mines. In spite of some enormous damage services were usually restored within forty-eight hours, but the greatest disruption was inevitably caused by the many unexploded bombs. The subsequent 'baby Blitz' hit the Met and the GCR in six places, and the war culminated in the seven serious attacks by the V1 'flying bombs' (August to December 1944) and three by the V2 rockets (September to March 1945).

Paddington (Praed Street) Station was bombed on 14 October 1940, killing six people waiting on the platforms. The scene is littered with wreckage, much of it from the arched roof, which has been badly damaged. An Engineers train is removing the debris. (*LTM*)

Above: During the night of 16 September 1940, the Kilburn and Brondesbury viaduct bridges of the Met and LNER were demolished by a high explosive bomb. Only able to work during daylight and using available materials, a temporary bridge was built so that the lines opened again some thirteen days later, and this picture was taken later on 2 October. (*LTM*)

Below: Towards the end of the war, conventional bombing gave way to the V1 'flying bombs' and then the V2 rockets. Marylebone Station had been badly bombed earlier and on 17 August a V1 landed on the throat of the station. The main signal box was destroyed but this picture shows it being rebuilt so that it was operational by 24 August. (*British Railways*)

By today's standards the speed with which repairs were performed, mainly by scarce manual effort and few mechanical aids, is quite remarkable. Indeed, so was the resilience of the staff who gave their all at such times whilst working long hours of overtime, serving in other organisations such as the Home Guard, and on meagre food rations. Inevitably, under these wartime pressures the old standards of routine track and locomotive maintenance became a lower priority, and after the war the Treasury was once again parsimonious in its settlement for wartime work. The resultant fragile finances of the railways and the large backlogs in repairs and maintenance that had accumulated were now to form a millstone to be inherited by BR.

As if these wars were not enough, there has unfortunately been an almost constant background of violent protest by agitators and terrorists of various kinds often targeting the vulnerable railways. The agitators have broadly been largely specific interest groups or individuals, whilst many terrorists have campaigned against Western values, seen by them to be decadent, in favour of their ideal of society. Independence was the motive that inspired terrorists of the Fenian Brotherhood of Irish Republicans, originating in America, who saw the railways as an ideal target.

On 30 October 1883 they used dynamite against a train leaving Praed Street for Edgware Road, injuring some sixty-two passengers (many with bad facial injuries due to the glass). On 2 January 1885 they again planted a bomb on a Met train which exploded in Gower Street (now Euston Square) Station. This was followed by their bombing of another Met train at Aldersgate (now Barbican) Station on 26 April 1897, injuring some ten passengers of whom two subsequently died.

Similar motives inspired the renewed IRA attacks after the Second World War with, amongst other targets, two bombs at Baker Street Station in August 1973 and three more in March 1976. Bombs were placed on Met trains at Harrow on the Hill and Neasden in December 1991 and, in 1993, the Bishopsgate bombing took place, severely damaging Liverpool Street Station.

Sadly the busy and confined spaces of the underground railways still represent attractive targets for terrorists and recently, on 7 July 2005, there were the bombings of LT trains at Edgware Road and near King's Cross, as well as other targets, due to Al-Qaeda-inspired ascetic objectives, causing severe disruption and loss of life.

However, back when the Met opened in 1863 the directors were not then unduly concerned about the damaging effects of war or terrorists on their success. Indeed they were far more apprehensive about the scare campaign that had been whipped up on the terrors of travelling underground at speed and in total darkness, hauled by a fire burning engine, emitting sulphurous fumes and likely to collide with another train! Inevitably the omnibus and cab owners lent their weight to this anxiety.

Whilst there certainly was a problem with the atmosphere in the tunnels, this was soon made tolerable by the condensing locomotives and extra airshafts. The Met also devoted considerable attention to achieving safe operation by employing the equivalent of railway policemen at each station to control train movements, thus a signalman today

Above: The Met has always been an attractive target for agitators and terrorists and the first major incidents were perpetrated by the Irish Fenians group, who undertook a sustained bombing campaign at the end of the nineteenth century. The first attack was in 1883 on a Met train leaving Praed Street for Edgware Road Station. (*Museum of London*)

Below: The second of the series of Fenian attacks was with dynamite placed on a Met train which exploded in Gower Street Station (now Euston Square) in January 1897. It caused considerable damage and was followed by another bombing of a Met train at Aldersgate (now Barbican) later in 1897. (*Museum of London*)

is still called a 'bobby'. Subsequently the GWR assisted with the provision of an advanced mechanical signalling system. The records show that in the first four and a half years the Met carried some 70 million passengers without accident to them.

Indeed, there were apparently relatively few fatal accidents involving the public on the Met in its entire history. Nevertheless, this is only part of the story, for the early engines were notoriously unreliable, and whilst the crews often performed incredible major running repairs to get to the next station, boiler failures did occur. In fact one of the Great Northern Railway engines on loan to the Met exploded in 1864, but it should be noted that in these incidents it was usually the Met staff who suffered and, in such a paternalistic regime, the pervading attitude was that it 'went with the job'.

The Met managed to avoid major accidents, but undoubtedly their operations were affected by continual difficulties due to high traffic levels causing maintenance and signalling problems. Here a T Stock set has run into the buffers at Moorgate and is being re-railed by manual effort and hydraulic jacks. (*John Parnham*)

Derailments were also common due to tight radius curves and buffers/couplings becoming locked. The Pullman cars were notorious for this problem. Here a T Stock set has jackknifed. (*John Parnham*)

A regular job (with a uniform) on the railway was prized, but all manual rail men were vulnerable to serious accident, from crews, shunters and porters to permanent way workers. It is salutary to find that the standard award to the family of an employee killed in service was £10 in comparison with an ad hoc compensation by the Board to an inconvenienced passenger of £100. In spite of this, there was a loyalty and comradeship across the employees, who responded to operating problems in taking responsibility for trying to provide a service. For example, the Met encouraged this by trying to allocate crews to the same locomotive in order to foster responsibility. To the same end activities such as station garden competitions, football teams and involvement in local activities were encouraged. Overall the picture is one of a very intensive train service run with limited funds and maintained by ingenuity and 'cannibalisation'. It was said at Neasden that the Met depended on 'scrap and luck'.

Of all the causes for accidents human actions and signalling mistakes were the main factors. Again, many of these were not overtly publicised and some of the signalling incidents occurred due to the friction between the signalmen arising from their different allegiances to the Met, GCR, LNER and LT staff and their retention of past employment conditions. One such 'failure of communication' resulted in an LNER express ending up in Harrow Goods Yard! With the absorption into LT in 1933, Pick imposed an overarching regime of safety and regulation, but with some inevitable loss of the flexibility and initiative that had been inherent with the Met.

CHAPTER SIX

THE POST-WAR ERA

The railway systems of most other European countries were so badly damaged by the Second World War that there was little option but to rebuild them to modern standards. However, although Britain had survived, it was impoverished and had learnt to maintain its own railways by means of a culture of 'make do and mend', which inevitably meant governments had to strike an unsatisfactory balance between maintaining a public service and having insufficient funding to improve its efficiency. Thus, the policy adopted by post-war governments has tended to swing like a pendulum between nationalisation and privatisation – neither of which have addressed the basic issue of under-funding.

NATIONALISATION

In that over sixty years have passed since the end of the Second World War, it is tempting to try to reflect on why – from that time of hope – more progress has not been made in improving our vital railway infrastructure, in particular the then Met & GC Joint Line. Indeed, many believe that there has been a decline in service. During this time the emphasis has swung between nationalisation and privatisation (including a number of hybrids) under governments of a variety of persuasions, yet the outcomes have been less than satisfactory. Therefore the problem appears to be more questions of priority and implementation.

Although the last war was won, it further exacerbated the basic problems revealed by the First World War, as Britain came to be in a precarious socio-economic situation. The cost of the war had virtually bankrupted the country, and the little money for investment that was available had to be used to try to just maintain the existing infrastructure rather than to enhance it. Due to the vast backlog in repair and maintenance it often amounted to little more than ad hoc repairs or the buying of existing (but virtually obsolete) equipment. Not only was the transport infrastructure and industry in a parlous state, the population was worn out by years of hardship and deprivation as well as facing the prospect of rationing continuing into the foreseeable future – in practice until 1956! Inevitably, this backdrop led to a strong desire for political change and thus Labour won a sweeping victory in 1945, with a strong mandate to nationalise most of the country's main providers of services, from transport, health and coal to the ports and docks, in order to improve their efficiency and public access. It was not only a question of 'big is best', but 'public ownership is even better'. Unfortunately this well-intentioned programme would lack the necessary funds to establish these nationalised bodies in the

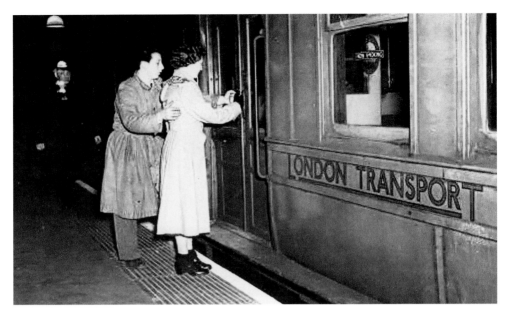

Seen here after the Second World War, the last run of the old wooden-bodied electric stock on the Inner Circle. At Aldgate Station on New Year's Eve 1950, a gallant young man is helping his girlfriend to open the double sliding doors to enter the train. (*LTM*)

Incredibly, this scene captured in 1953 at Whitechapel Station on the East London Line could have been taken over twenty years earlier. An old H stock train, soon to disappear, is entering the unchanged station past one of the original Met diamond-shaped red, white and blue name boards. (*David T. Bosher*)

proper manner, let alone invest in the future. Indeed, the new Government soon had to beg the United State of America for a loan even to maintain the status quo! This was grudgingly given, on condition that Empire trading preferences were restricted, and with onerous terms which meant that repayments were only completed in 1996!

Also relevant to the story of post-war recovery of the railways is the fact that their multiplicity of associated equipment suppliers were in a similar parlous state. Having been diverted to manufacturing armaments it was natural to revert to making variants of pre-war designs, and then to the requirements of the newly nationalised body. The rest of the world had moved on, however, and was seeking advanced designs that were more reliable, with new motive power, at prices that could only be achieved by large volume production. This has led to the demise of most well-known UK manufacturers and their replacement by those from overseas.

The railway companies mounted strong opposition to nationalisation, which forced the Government to increase compensation to such a generous level that they were pre-pared to accept the inevitable. So the 1947 Transport Act came into force on 1 January 1948, with the British Transport Commission taking over most of the rail, bus, tram, canal and road distribution services. The existing railways were grouped together on an arbitrary regional basis and came under the British Railways Executive (BRE), whilst LT became the London Transport Executive, with other executives created for Hotels, Docks and Waterways and Road Transport. Whilst in many ways this was a logical structure, it nevertheless contained ambiguities that bedevilled progress for the next forty years.

These fundamental flaws relate to the uncertainties over the objectives of the Commission as to the extent of providing a universal public service and at what profit or loss. Inevitably from these questions followed that of who was actually responsible – the Ministry of Transport, the Department of Trade and Industry, the Treasury, the BRE or LT? In that all had a vested interest, they could all interfere if they thought fit or otherwise 'pass the parcel', and this was made worse by the nature of the players and a frequently changing political landscape. So the consequence of these basic ambigui-ties, when combined with the shortage of funds for investment in capital projects, was a recipe for disaster.

The practical constraints are illustrated by the fact that the size of the BRE alloca-tion for the whole LT capital expenditure in post-war years was sometimes as low as £300,000 per annum. Indeed, the asset value of LT actually decreased during this period. It has been the convoluted processes of approval, monitoring and review by numerous bodies leading to uncertainty, indecision and lack of confidence that has so often preju-diced the outcomes from even the modest sums made available.

The extent of such uncertainties is indicated by the number of changes in nominal 'ownership' of the ex-LT and ex-LNER lines that worked the Joint in the period of nationalisation covered in the next chapter. LT had some six 'owners', eventually with a radical shift from the BRE to the Greater London Council (GLC) under Ken Livingstone (1981). Whilst these changes were going on, the lines from Marylebone which started by being in Eastern Region (1948) were moved to the Western Region (1950) and then to the London Midland Region (1958). Such change, seemingly for change's sake, reveals an inability to face up to the basic problems and actually made the situation worse.

Thus, the main factors which are even now still contributing to an unsatisfactory record in capital infrastructure projects are: the lack of clear and consistent objectives and responsibilities for the railway companies; an unstable political environment mainly interested in results within the lifetime of the government, thus leading to continual changes in government attitude; and ad hoc policies often influenced by local political factors. Uncertainty also arises from continual reviews of projects analogous to 'pulling up a plant to see how the roots are doing' – with the inevitable negative effect on the plant! The Treasury control techniques on investment, such as 'annularity', which are used to minimise spending, also create a lack of confidence in the future of a project.

As if these factors were not enough to prejudice progress, it often seems as if that familiar spectre to successful project completion – the 'Law of Unintended Consequences' – comes into action! This highlights the situation that occurs when a project is moving satisfactorily to meet its objective, but the whole premise of the task is negated by a dramatic change in the reasons for its existence. For example, due to shortages of coal, the major BR programme to convert steam locomotives to burn oil and build the necessary refuelling depots was scrapped when oil prices subsequently rose, making the scheme unviable.

The impact of the above factors, unfortunately, has been apparent on most of the major post-war investment programmes in the railways from the Victoria Line, the upgrade to the West Coast Main Line and now to CrossRail, where the delays and consequent increase in costs have been horrendous. Against this background it is appropriate to review the actual train services over the Joint by the LT and BRE.

MET SERVICES OF LONDON TRANSPORT

As far as the lines that this book is primarily concerned with, nationalisation meant that the Met & GCJ ceased to exist at the end of 1947 after a separate existence of some forty-one years. The last Joint Committee meeting was chaired by Butler-Henderson of the LNER (and ex-GCR), and during it Lord Ashfield resigned and stated that he was also resigning as Chairman of LT. He died the next year. From 1948 the operation of these lines would now be shared between two new subsidiaries of the BTC (British Transport Commission) – LT and the Eastern Region of BR – if only for a short period of time, for both were to be continually transmuted into different forms over the years of public ownership.

The BRE's view of such inherited joint operations was that the undertaking should be transferred to the main user, and so by 1950 LT was given responsibility for Harrow South to Aylesbury South, whilst north of Aylesbury Station went to Eastern Region. Now no LT trains ran north of the renamed station of Aylesbury Town. In addition, whereas responsibilities for signalling and maintenance had been split near Great Missenden, now LT took control to Aylesbury. However, the complexities of the Joint were not to be brushed aside so easily and, as the steam to electric changeover still took place at Rickmansworth, the old rule books had to apply.

Equally, many of the day-to-day activities from revenue sharing to goods handling still relied on the rules of the Joint Agreement so that the previous liaison continued much as before. Even so, it was all a bit of surprise to the British Railways (Eastern Region), particularly when they found that the ex-Joint staff had 'protected status' which precluded transferring them to other lines! Whilst as before the operations of the LT/Met and the BR/Marylebone lines remained inextricably linked, nationalisation was to have a profound impact in different ways on each of them.

The first problem that the incoming nationalised LT faced was the need to rapidly improve the facilities for the 1948 Olympic Games at Wembley and the 'flat junction' track layouts south and north of Harrow. Beyond this there was little financial scope for capital investment. However, by 1950 a review of the suspended pre-war New Works Programme for electrifying north of Rickmansworth had shown that in practice a lot of the civil engineering had already been completed. Then, with economies from re-aligning the existing tracks, some simplification of the junction to Watford and abandoning the intentions for Chorleywood, Rickmansworth, Pinner and North Harrow Stations a more cost-effective proposal for £3.5 million could be put forward to the Ministry of Transport who had taken direct responsibility for LT in 1953.

By the end of the 1950s, the ex-Met Class E & F steam engines of LT were becoming uneconomic to maintain and they started to look for replacements. The Class F 0-6-2Ts were the last built to meet the loading gauge of the tunnels south of Finchley Road and here No.L50 is taking a Permanent Way train on to Neasden Depot. (*David T. Bosher*)

By 1960 work had restarted on the pre-war plans to quadruple the tracks to Rickmansworth and electrify beyond to Chesham and Amersham. Here, the primitive North Harrow Station, with bridge and ground to the west of the existing tracks are being prepared for the additional lines. The fine pediment proclaiming the M&GCJ ownership carved over the North Harrow Station has been removed. (*LTM*)

During the war the Chesham Shuttle of an E Class Tank plus Dreadnought coaches was replaced by ex-GCR Class locomotives and old Ashbury coaches fitted for auto working, so that the complex operation of the engine having to run round the train was avoided. At the end of the war, Ken Palmer, the fireman, is alongside LNER Class 9K No. 5193 at the primitive Chesham coaling platform. (*Ron White*)

LT remained pessimistic that such a programme would go ahead and continued to explore other ways of economising on the extremities of the Met. To this end they collaborated with BR on trials to replace the Chesham Shuttle with a three-car set of ACV lightweight 125 hp diesel rail bus. It ran for some two weeks in October 1953 with the usual C13 tank engine in attendance as a back-up, and although this was not called upon it was apparent that the rail buses were struggling with the sharp bends and were unable to cope with any goods wagons, so they were passed on for trials elsewhere on BR.

Although the £3.5 million proposition for the electrification represented the largest request by the London Transport Executive for many years, it nevertheless received strong support from Eastern Region and, somewhat surprisingly, against the track record of the funding of other LTE projects, it was approved in 1956. Work progressed well, and after trials with Met T stock multiple units the new lines opened on 12 September 1960. Unfortunately there were considerable delays in the delivery of the new A60 multiple electric stock, and so the old T stock continued whilst the fast trains were hauled by the stalwart Bo-Bo locomotives. The steam-operated Chesham Shuttle continued operating until 12 September 1960.

The new A60 ('A' for Amersham) multiple electric stock ordered for the line from Cravens had their origins in the pre-war Acton designs, employing sliding doors, through gangways (for safety in tunnels) and a higher proportion of space for the standing passengers on the Inner London sector. After the war, from 1947 to 1953, two variants of this concept (Nos. 17000 and 20000) were trialled, with the experimental saloon-type bodies mounted on old T stock underframes. Then some 248 A60 cars in four-car sets were ordered from Cravens, with the last being delivered in 1963. A further 216 of an interchangeable design were then ordered, primarily for the Uxbridge line.

The light aluminium alloy body and sub-frame were mounted on a steel underframe, and both of the axles of the end cars were motorised. Recognising the different performance required over the diverse sections of the Met, the controls gave the option of high acceleration for the Inner Circle or a higher speed of 60mph for the surface lines. Also, the power of the carriage heaters had been doubled to cope with the bleak winter weather over the Chilterns, but as might be expected the new saloon stock met with much criticism from die-hard *Metro-land* commuters.

The initial complaints were that the seating capacity had been reduced from the 600 of a T stock train to some 464 on the A60s and that the luggage racks were inadequate. But as time went by it was the hard seats, bad riding and pitching motion that the passengers resented, and this led to an ongoing preference whenever possible to travelling by the alternative gentler Marylebone trains with better upholstery, heating and also toilets.

The electrification, new track layouts and A60 stock enabled roughly 50 per cent more train services to be operated and with faster timing. As might be expected the reductions were minimal for the Uxbridge line, but for Amersham the journey time to Baker Street was lowered from fifty to forty-one minutes. At the time this appeared greater to passengers because they had suffered from even longer journeys during the electrification work. The older and cynical *Metro-landers* recalled that formerly the Met did the journey in forty-five minutes.

Another view of the Chesham Shuttle with the Ashbury coaches in the platform. Originally 1898 steam stock, these had been converted to electric traction (hence the drivers windows) before being placed in the strategic reserve prior to the war, and then converted back to steam operation for the Shuttle. The C13 tank engine has uncoupled to shunt wagons or take on coal. (*C.A.F. Coll*)

The 'through' Met trains from the City were hauled at speed by swaying Bo-Bo electric locos to Rickmansworth, where there was a slick changeover to steam traction for the rest of the journey. This was often the lot of tired ex-LNER Class N5 0-6-2Ts and on 12 April 1947 No.9257 leaves Rickmansworth bound for Chesham. (*C.A.F. Coll*)

When LT came under the control of the GLC in 1970, with its various political factions often at odds with the current governments, the Met was not a priority. At the operating level the search for the optimum train schedules continued, with the long-standing interplay of frequency of fast and stopping trains the consequences for the Inner Circle and the increasingly vociferous lobbies of commuters on the Uxbridge, Watford and particularly Amersham and Chesham lines. The latter were particularly resentful that their new bay platform had never been used to increase the frequency of the Shuttle, that there was little apparent attempt to synchronise it with the Marylebone trains at Chalfont & Latimer, and, as ever, this was tinged with the traditional belief that Amersham trains were given preference!

In the post-war era, the Chesham Shuttle continued to be provided by three ageing auto-working Met Ashbury coaches hauled by ex-GCR Class C13 tank engines. This 1955 Chesham scene is almost timeless, apart from the engine number revealing the preceding '6' added by BR. In 1957 responsibility for traction passed to the LMR who used a wide variety of LMS and BR engines until steam haulage for LT ceased on 12 September 1960. (*C.A.F. Coll*)

During the first week of operation of the electrified Chesham branch in September 1960, the old Met T stock is used for the 'Shuttle', whilst the previous steam 'Shuttle' waits in the new bay in case of its replacement's failure. Meanwhile, that daily pick-up goods train waits its turn. (*LTM*)

Left: From Wembley Park, looking towards Neasden power station during 1962 when all the new A60 stock had been delivered. From left to right: an eight-car set of A60s on the Met service to Baker Street; two red 1938 Bakerloo stock trains for Elephant & Castle and Wembley Park respectively; a four-car set of A60s going to form the Chesham Shuttle; and a similar eight-car set bound for Uxbridge. (*LTM*)

Opposite below: Even the new A60 stock had to suffer the idiosyncrasies of the Chesham branch, when a van being loaded with hay from a field near a bridge at Chesham Bois ran away and went down the embankment in front of the Chesham-bound Shuttle. The trains were severely delayed but nobody was injured. (*Ron White*)

By the 1970s their overriding concern was that even with the 40 per cent rise in fares that had taken place, LT claimed that the outer Met lines were losing £1.5 million per annum. This was alleviated in the 1980s with subsidies of £0.5 million per annum from public bodies, and now that Ken Livingstone had become leader of the GLC, his new 'fares fair' policy substantially lowered ticket prices for a time. Nevertheless, the Cheshamites were worried by the many financial reviews of the viability of the Met, for it was apparent that their branch was vulnerable.

Attempts were made to economise by eliminating trains on Sundays as well as other changes, but these were reinstated after protests. Then, in 1982, LT found that the original bridges over the River Chess into Chesham were unsafe and that neither they nor the local councils could afford the cost of £1.2 million for the necessary replacements. After that LT made a half-hearted proposal to terminate the branch on the outskirts of the town (ironically where Watkin had initially proposed to build his station until the inhabitants raised £2,000 to pay for the station to be in the town!).

Above: Due to lack of funds to replace the weakened bridges over the River Chess At Chesham, LT proposed again to terminate the branch at The Moor on the outskirts of the town! Fortunately at the eleventh hour support came from the GLC Residuary Body. The new single span bridge was erected alongside the old and slid into place on 24 March 1986. (*C.A.F. Coll*)

Above: The classic changeover between steam and electric traction at Rickmansworth continued until LT had sufficient A60 stock to operate to Amersham and Chesham. The time for this complex manoeuvre was under four minutes and here the Bo-Bo electric has just arrived from Baker Street and is pulling off to run back on the up line, to take the next train back. (*Dewi Williams*)

Below: Next an ex-LNER LT engine has come out of its siding and is about to be coupled to the train of Dreadnought coaches, before its stiff climb over the Chilterns. This routine had been performed for thirty-five years and was undertaken with an appearance of nonchalant professionalism that seemed almost balletic precision! (*Dewi Williams*)

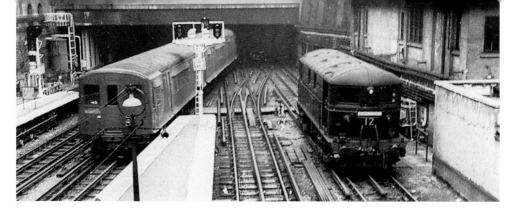

Above: March 1961: the scene at the throat to Baker Street Station before the new A60 stock came to dominate the services. The red O stock train is leaving for Uxbridge whilst ex-Met Bo–Bo electric locomotive No.17 *Florence Nightingale* waits in the siding. The pit in that siding was once used for servicing the Met steam engines. (*53A Models of Hull Coll*)

Above: The last scheduled train to Amersham of ex-Met Dreadnought coaches and a Bo–Bo electric locomotive ran on 26 May 1963. Surrounded by an admiring crowd, No.5 *John Hampden* (once of Wendover) is backing on to return the train back to Baker Street. Soon most of these locomotives were scrapped, apart from Nos 5 and 12. (*John Gillman*)

Below: With the demise of BR steam traction, their diesel locomotives began to appear, from shunters at Aylesbury to Class 24s on the Watford goods trip. In a snowy December of 1981, LT explored the possible use of a BR Class 25 diesel and here No.25306 is pausing during a clearance test, in the bay at Rickmansworth Station. (*LTM*)

When they were thirty-five years old, the LT A60 stock were refurbished by ABB and this picture in May 1996 at Chalfont & Latimer Station shows a BR Class 37 diesel locomotive hauling one of the eight-car sets to their Derby works. A match wagon is marshalled between the locomotive and the LT stock to accommodate the different couplings. (*Ron Potter*)

To replace the ageing ex-Met steam engines, in 1951 LT began to acquire some ex-GWR 0-6-0Ts. One of their duties was taking the daily rubbish train to the Tip at Watford. Here in June 1958, such an engine in LT maroon livery has run round its train at Watford and is approaching the access to the Tip via the South curve from Croxley. (*Les Reason*)

The ex-GW panniers operated the last scheduled steam services over the old Met lines. This LT engine, No.L95 (former GW No.5764) was withdrawn in 1971, but one of its last duties was hauling the Neasden steam breakdown crane set back to the Depot. (*David T. Bosher*)

Again Ken Livingstone saved the day for, just as the GLC was abolished, as their leader he persuaded the Residuary Body to pay for new bridges on the grounds that the main users were people who worked in London! These were built in 1986. As a further cost-saving measure, single-person operation was introduced in 1986, but the considerable cost of the re-wiring needed to remove the guard's position meant that some stock only had a partial modification which restricted their inter-operability.

With the demise of the GLC in 1980, LT became London Regional Transport in 1988, directly reporting to the Ministry of Transport, and soon their railway activities were segregated as London Underground Ltd. Now the main concern of Met travellers was becoming the unreliability of the service. This was due to a combination of factors: the track was causing problems and the maximum speed had to be reduced to 50mph; the ageing signalling, particularly between Baker Street and Harrow, was increasingly prone to failure at peak times; and in the autumn falling leaves on the more exposed sections were causing slipping and also poor electrical contact, affecting the signalling system.

The former factors were the result of the continuing underinvestment and the latter was mainly due to allowing the trackside foliage to grow unchecked, whereas during the Met era it was one of the many responsibilities of the permanent way gang to keep this under control. Several outlandish mechanical devices were tried out to clear the leaves, but without success, and so four minutes were added to journey times in the autumn to allow for such delays.

The 1990s brought winds of political change which were to turn into a hurricane for the railways, but for now it was very much a case of trying to maintain the status quo on a limited budget.

MARYLEBONE SERVICES OF BRITISH RAILWAYS

During nationalisation the BR services over the Joint Line were also to be subject to several changes of control. Whereas at senior level in LT most of the managers retained their posts during the continual changes, at BR the situation was worse than at the 'grouping' in 1923. In attempting to impose standardisation across BR and create the new regions, there was much jostling between the potential candidates. Inevitably they favoured their own traditions, but this could lead to much resentment. It often seemed that the choices were deliberately provocative in order to breakdown the inbred cultures of some of the 'Big Four'.

At the highest level, such as Chief Mechanical Engineer, these appointments were to have a profound effect on the implementation of standardisation. As might be expected, the imposition of BR created a new level of bureaucracy and, somewhat ironically, their headquarters were located at the former Great Central Hotel in 222 Marylebone Road, which was given the indicative nickname of 'The Kremlin'!

The first impact of BR standardisation on the rolling stock was the trial of various new liveries and, briefly, one of the venerable and dirty C13 tank engines reappeared on the Chesham Shuttle in apple green carrying the words 'BRITISH RAILWAYS' on the sides of its water tanks. This phase ended with a trend to revert to using black for most engines and green for the more important express types, although the different regions, particularly the Western, often liked to demonstrate their independence in this matter. The BR logo and a new BR-wide locomotive numbering scheme was applied, achieved by simply applying a prefix to the existing number. In the case of the former LNER stock, which somewhat confusingly had just been renumbered preceding nationalisation, it was achieved by now adding the prefix '6'. The new livery for corridor coaches became known as 'plum and custard', but eventually the standard finish in most regions for all coaches became Midland red.

Until BR could tackle the extremely contentious issue of producing their own standard designs of rolling stock for the future, existing types originating from the 'Big Four' (and even some new developments) continued to be produced by the Regions. As an input to the design of the forthcoming BR standard locomotives, in 1948 comparative trials were held between the leading contenders from the 'Big Four'. The tests on the mixed traffic locomotives were performed over the Joint Line from Marylebone between a GWR 'Hall', a SR 'West Country' and a LMS 'Black 5'. There was no representative from the LNER, as it was assumed that the performance of the 'home' engines was well understood.

It is interesting to note, however, that in the other trials between heavy freight locomotives, Robinson's 2-8-0 design of 1911 for the GCR did well against even the recent WD 2-8-0 and 2-10-0s produced for the Government during the war. With unfamiliar coal and routes, as well as crews with different objectives, it is not surprising that the results of all the trials, including this set, were ambiguous and did not suggest an 'ideal' design. So BR proceeded to produce their own standard designs of steam locomotives which were rapidly made obsolete by a fresh BR policy to 'dash for diesel' traction. Again BR acted too impetuously by ordering some twenty-five different varieties of diesel locomotives from virtually all of the UK suppliers, few of which turned out to be suitable or reliable. A second generation proved better and included the InterCity High Speed Trains which revolutionised the express passenger services.

As might be expected, at first the LNER passed the reins for the services from Marylebone to the Eastern Region of BR, and so the services and locomotives over the Joint remained much the same. Although the war was over, the standards of cleaning and maintenance continued to decline, and even those engines returning from major overhauls with their fresh BR numbers and logos were soon reduced to a uniform layer of grime. It was sad to see the once proud ex-GCR Directors with such resonant names reduced to this state. The only exception seemed to be the new LNER 2-6-4T locomotives, designed by Edward Thompson and designated as Class L1 (causing the existing ex-GCR Class to become L3s), which were not greatly thought of by the conservative Neasden crews. Otherwise locals were hauled by Classes A5, C13, N5 and N7, whilst fast trains continued with the usual ex-GCR types plus A3, B1 and V2s.

In 1958 BR instituted yet another major organisational change, with responsibility for the services from Marylebone passing to the Western Region! This decision was possibly influenced by the GW&GCJ Line services, but as the complexity of what they had inherited was realised they rapidly shed some of their responsibilities. Whilst Western Region retained control of Marylebone-Harrow, Eastern Region stock continued to provide the service, except that the London Midland Region became responsible for goods and parcels.

Following the creation of British Railways in 1948, all locomotives were given a BR insignia and (apart from the GWR) renumbered by a prefix '6' in the case of the LNER. Here in 1949, No.69315 an ex-Parker Class N5 0-6-2T undertakes the daily coal train run from Harrow along the Uxbridge branch. (*C.R.L. Coles*)

Above: To tap the lucrative traffic for the Wembley Exhibition, the LNER built a loop line from the GC line on the GW&GC route to enable their trains to run a convenient service to Marylebone from within the complex. It remained popular for stadium events, and this shows an ex-LNER Class A5 in the late 1940s with such a train on the loop. (*C.R.L. Coles*)

Above: Under BR, responsibility for the Joint Line was moved between their various regions – particularly the Eastern and Midland. This resulted in a wide range of rolling stock appearing on the route, here typified by No.90080, an ex-wartime Ministry of Supply 2-8-0, designed by Riddles of the LMS, whose ideas were the basis of the post-war BR designs. Here it is ambling through Rickmansworth with a Neasden Goods. (*S. Gradidge*)

Above: At this time ER reintroduced named expresses from Marylebone and here an up *Master Cutler* from Sheffield is passing Rickmansworth Goods Yard, headed by a Gresley Class A3 4-6-2 No.60049 *Prince Palatine*. In the yard a Thompson Class L1 No.67784 is shunting wagons for the daily freight to Quainton Road. (*L. V. Reason*)

Opposite below: In 1955 work to replace a bridge over Regent's Park Canal resulted in Met trains being diverted into Marylebone Station. This shows one of these trains of Dreadnought coaches, headed and tailed by Thompson Class L1 2-6-4T engines, departing Rickmansworth, past the Met Goods Depot. (*L. V. Reason*)

As time passed, in practice passengers saw little change until some pre-war prestige passenger services over the ex-GCR were revived and the underutilised Marylebone was used for new and diverted services. Thus, night newspaper and mail trains continued and were joined by two named expresses, the *South Yorkshireman* and the *Master Cutler*, which found favour in comparison with the less reliable services from St Pancras. Then work on rebuilding Euston led to the diversion of the popular cheap Scottish car transporters and to other specials using Marylebone. These changes led to the appearance of a number of LMR locomotives in addition to more A3s and V2s for the heavier trains over the ex-GC, and this time represented the apogee of post-war steam over the Joint.

This was about to change once more however, for in 1958 control of the ex-GC routes passed to the Midland Region. To many, their subsequent actions were mainly motivated by the past rivalry between their predecessor, the Midland Railway, and the Great Central. Certainly they moved to eliminate competition to their own route to the Midlands from St Pancras and a gradual process began of downgrading the Marylebone services. The named trains and expresses were cancelled at the start of 1960 and just three inconvenient semi-fast trains substituted. Most cross-country trains were withdrawn by 1963 and the local stations north of Aylesbury had nearly all been closed.

In a pristine BR livery during the mid-1950s, a Thompson Class B1 4-6-0 No.61187 hauls an up express for Marylebone approaching Great Missenden. These locomotives were much liked by the London Division footplate crews. (*L. V. Reason*)

During this period of decline the motive power for the longer turns was mainly worn-out Black 5s, Britannias and even Baby Scots – one of which was mistakenly diverted with the daily pick-up goods onto the Chesham branch thereby causing much consternation! Until electrification, the Shuttle itself was operated by Ivatt 2MT 2-6-2T locomotives which were auto-fitted to work with the existing Ashbury coaches. Other local services from Marylebone via Rickmansworth were hauled by a succession of equally worse for wear BR Class 2MT and 4MT tank engines built by Fowler, Stanier, Ivatt and Fairburn, plus the occasional 4MT 2-6-0 tender locomotive. Another indication of the sorry state of things was the transfer of the base for the motive power to Willesden and the closure of Neasden engine shed in 1962.

But in the background the various governments' concerns over the rising losses of BR led to a series of reviews that had a fundamental impact on BR and, in particular, the lines from Marylebone. The BTC had unveiled its modernisation plans in 1955 which initiated spending over £1 billion to replace steam by diesel and electric traction. In the haste to implement this policy much money was wasted in ordering a plethora of designs, so that many were scrapped after relatively short lives. This was followed by two notorious reports by Dr Beeching, the first in 1963 recommending that some third of all lines – mainly cross-country and branch lines – should be closed, whilst the second in 1964 proposed rationalisation of the main lines.

Needless to say, the acceptance and implementation of these reports considerably weakened the prospects for Marylebone. The end was now in sight for steam trains over the Joint, with the closure of many signal boxes and the withdrawal of freight services in 1963. The last scheduled steam train ran to Nottingham on 3 September 1966. The recently introduced BR Derby-built Class 115 diesel-powered multiple units now operated all the local Marylebone services.

Above: The other ER 'titled' train that ran for a period over the Joint in the 1950s was the *South Yorkshireman* from Bradford. Just arrived at Aylesbury Town Station for Marylebone, is ex–LNER Gresley Pacific Class A3 No.60049 *Galtee More*, taking water and framed by a fine array of semaphore signals. (*L. V. Reason*)

Above: Another Gresley ex-LNER locomotive (a 2-6-0 Class K3 No.61842) which was based on an earlier GNR design, is heading an up semi-fast from Nottingham. This view highlights the tight restricting curve through Rickmansworth, which was due to a Director of the Bank of England being unwilling to sell his land to the right of the picture. (*L. V. Reason*)

Below: The somewhat ramshackle Moor Park (& Sandy Lodge) Station was built in 1910 to serve the an exclusive Golf Club and housing development. Here, almost 50 years later, little has changed, except there is a frequent electric train service to Watford and Rickmansworth, together with the shaking of the wooden structure by expresses such as this Gresley Class V2 thundering through for Marylebone. (*S. Gradidge*)

Above: Another up *Master Cutler* express, headed by a Gresley *4-6-2* Class A3 locomotive No.60104 *Solaro* gently easing round the curve at Rickmansworth Station with its standard BR *'blood & custard'* liveried coaches towards Marylebone, around 1955. (*S. Gradidge*)

Above: Continual reorganisations by BR meant that the Joint moved from Eastern to Western and then in 1958 to Midland Region control. Inevitably ex-LMS locomotives now dominated the schedules and here a Stanier Jubilee No.45735 *Comet*, rebuilt with double-chimney and larger boiler to be upgraded to Class 7P, has left Rickmansworth with an up stopping train in 1959. (*S. Gradidge*)

Below: Unsurprisingly, the Midland Region favoured their own routes from St Pancras and so the Joint/London Extension services were steadily run down. In the summer of 1960 *Royal Welsh Fusilier*, a Fowler Royal Scot class 4-6-0 rebuilt by Stanier in 1942 with a taper boiler and double chimney nears Amersham bound for Marylebone. (*S. Gradidge*)

Equally, the steam-hauled Met services were also gradually taken over by pre-nationalisation LMS tank engines. This shows an up slow passenger train from Woodford Halse pulling out of Rickmansworth. The locomotive is an LMS Fairburn No.42231 2-6-4T Class 4 of 1945 which was based on a much earlier design by Fowler. (*S. Gradidge*)

In 1963 the overarching BTC was abolished and BR began to divide the control of operations on the basis of service provision, such as the InterCity expresses. Thus the services from Marylebone became part of Network South East and, with the ongoing growth of housing development in Bucks and the good DMU services, the number of commuters began to steadily increase. Yet the legacy of Beeching meant that there was still unease at BR. Certainly for its capacity Marylebone was still underutilised, and it was realised that the value of the whole site for redevelopment was attractive to the impoverished BR.

Sir David Serpell was then commissioned by the Thatcher Government to look at further 'Beeching style' reductions in the railway network, and in particular in 1983 he recommended the closure of Marylebone and the conversion of the tracks into high-speed bus routes. Existing GW&GC services were to be diverted into Paddington and those using the Met & GC Joint Line would be provided with extra services into Baker Street. This proposal was well received by the BR accountants and soon posters appeared warning that stations would be closed on 15 March 1984.

As might be expected this provoked strong and vociferous objections from the commuters who would be affected. Years of protesting over problems with their trains had brought them to such a state of annoyance that this news raised their anger to an organised level that was not expected by BR. At the same time, the realities of Serpell's somewhat naive proposals began to be questioned not only by commuters but by middle managers at BR and LT too. Firstly, as subsequent experience has shown, the conversion of railways to roads is difficult and expensive due to the clearances involved. Second, with the growth in passenger numbers mentioned earlier, both Baker Street and also Paddington lacked the necessary extra capacity. As a result, BR reversed its decision, and the notice of closures was withdrawn on 30 April 1986 to much celebration throughout the length of *Metro-land*!

A new Chairman of BR, Bob Reid, scrapped the previous feudal regional organisation and applied the business model of clearly identifiable and accountable units, each with their own objectives and resources. The success of this action was confirmed by the performance of Network South East (NSE) which was led by the dynamic Chris Green (who had earlier created the successful InterCity business) and who further separated out the Marylebone services of NSE under the brand 'Chiltern Line' – with their own logo – and soon the quality of service and passengers numbers increased.

Indeed Bob Reid was so impressed that he agreed to Chris Green's next step of turning the Chiltern Line into a modern railway. This was made easier because the Chiltern Line had little interaction with other parts of BR and could be re-equipped with new DMUs offering higher standards of passenger comfort, upgraded track, new signalling based on an Automatic Train Protection system and revamped stations, including the Marylebone flagship. The key to realising this plan would be the appointment of a BR colleague, namely Adrian Shooter, as the new manager of the Chiltern Line.

Gradually the dominance by LMS engines was diluted by the emergence of the standard BR designs (although many showed a strong LMS influence!). Here an Ivatt designed 2-6-0 Class 4 built in 1947 is shunting in Rickmansworth yard, where the cut-away tender gave good visibility for reverse running. (*S. Gradidge*)

By the time this picture was taken in 1960, this BR standard 4-6-0 Class 5 No.73032 which had only been built in 1952 already looks worn and uncared for. This reflects the difficulty of maintaining all the locomotive stock as well as the low priority of the London Extension. The train at Rickmansworth is an up coal delivery for Neasden. (*S. Gradidge*)

Above: Soon after the Met electrification to Amersham in 1961, a number of expresses were diverted over the Joint when Euston Station was being rebuilt. The deteriorating state of BR steam engines is shown by the condition of one of their prestigious Britannia Class 4-6-0's No.70014 *Iron Duke*, leaking steam as it limps through Chorleywood. (*S. Gradidge*)

Below: Apart from bringing a wide variety of different engines over the Joint, this sunset of steam services was a sad time. Increasingly, the ubiquitous Stanier 4-6-0s (or *Black Fives*) took over the dwindling services until one hauled the last train on the 3 September 1966. Here earlier that year is No.44916 on an up semi-fast approaching Amersham. (*S. Gradidge*)

Above left: First in BR green livery, then blue and later in Network Southeast and Chiltern Line colours, BR Derby-built Class 115 DMUs took over the Marylebone–Aylesbury services and regenerated the prospects for the line. In 1960, with the LT quadrupling and electrification work in progress, an up DMU approaches Moor Park with an extra van and coach. (*E. Gadsden*)

Above right: In 1989 the Centenary of the opening of the Chesham branch was celebrated in fine style, the highlight being the running of the restored original MET 1 E Class locomotive from Chesham to Watford. Such was the success that for a number of years annual steam trains were run over the Met, often with relevant engines. Here at Amersham in 1993 are L90 &L99, two ex-GWR Pannier tanks (7760 & 7715) in their final LT liveries. (*C.A.F. Coll*)

By 1991 all these upgrades had been completed, together with a new integrated electronic control centre at Marylebone which managed the system and a maintenance base at Aylesbury for the new Class 165 Network Turbo DMUs which had replaced the ageing Class 115s. The whole programme cost some £65 million, and the results were evident in the superior ride and comfort of the new DMUs, which led to an increase in passengers and also encouraged new services and consideration of reopening the longer distance services on the old GW&GC.

Whilst in many ways the Chiltern Line was self-contained and thus somewhat isolated from the rest of BR, inevitably it continued, as always, to potentially conflict with the LT operations. As with the Class 115 DMUs, sharing the same track was solved by fitting LT-type tripcocks to the new Turbos to achieve compatibility with their signalling system, but the long-standing issues of revenue sharing and responsibility for delays continued.

Being virtually a separate entity within BR, in many ways the Chiltern Line project was the forerunner of the next phase of evolution of the UK railways, but it is instructive to consider the basic faults in the nationalisation concept that had been adopted. In retrospect, the analysis by Beeching was based on the viability of individual stations over just a few days and did not reflect the role of branch lines as 'feeders' of freight and passengers to the trunk routes.

Equally, the rationalisation of those trunk routes which involved closures and 'singling' tracks was another short-term solution. It was implemented at a time when motorway construction was a popular policy, but now, with major concerns over fuel shortages, energy conservation, global warming and the environment, railways present a relatively attractive method of transport. Indeed, some branches have been reopened, double tracks restored and modern rolling stock introduced, leading to more passengers being carried than since the last war!

CHAPTER SEVEN

A SORT OF PRIVATISATION

During her period of office, Mrs Thatcher gave the impression of tolerating the railways as 'a necessary evil', and, as with other nationalised industries, she was more interested in passing responsibility to the private sector by way of privatisation. Probably the only one of her actions that had a positive outcome for the future potential of the UK railways was signing the agreement with President Mitterrand of France in 1984 to build the Channel Tunnel, which opened in 1994. Needless to say, this was mainly done for political reasons and, even then, only if funded mainly by the private sector.

Whilst the more tractable nationalised industries such as gas, water, coal, telecommunications and hcity were soon privatised, some others, including the Royal Mail and BR, presented inherent problems which made them a lower priority. Indeed it was not until John Major subsequently came to power that proposals to privatise BR were developed.

Interestingly, it is said that the prime minister personally favoured a structure resembling the 'Big Four' of pre-war days but unfortunately was persuaded to adopt the wider competition offered by a separation into train operating companies, infrastructure and a multiplicity of support businesses. In the event he lost the 1997 election, but the incoming Labour Government, who had previously declared that they would stop the privatisation, performed a volte-face, and, much to the annoyance of the unions, embraced the basic legislation.

It was implemented in 1998 with the core British Rail infrastructure vested in Railtrack, with the addition of strategic and regulatory oversight. Private companies competed for the twenty-five route franchises to become Train Operating Companies, and these TOCs mainly hired their rolling stock from various leasing companies. These in turn were to acquire their initial stock from British Rail on very favourable terms, and afterwards directly from the manufacturers. Outsourcing was much encouraged so that Railtrack and each of the main players relied on a raft of sub-contractors.

The net outcome as far as the passengers and freight customers were concerned was mixed. On the one hand, some TOCs were able to improve services and introduce new trains so that passenger numbers increased, but this was accompanied by greater complexity in ticketing, timetabling and anything involving co-operation between the often competing operators. Equally, whilst there was real competition over the profitable trunk routes, the less-used ones suffered to the extent that some TOCs only ran one train a week on such routes in order to satisfy their contractual obligations.

Whilst grand strategic plans were launched for modernising the rail network, in practice, within the subsidy made available by the Government, Railtrack's priorities became limited to upgrades to existing lines and an ever-increasing battle to maintain the existing ageing network. In this, the inefficiency of having to work through a plethora of sub-contractors and the many other interested parties contributed to a series of serious accidents: Southall (1997); Ladbroke Grove (1999); Hatfield (2000) and Potters Bar (2002). This led in the end to Railtrack being forced into administration by the Government.

The Department for Transport took back the strategic and regulatory roles, and in 2002 created a new infrastructural body – Network Rail – which would take more direct control of its work. Network Rail is funded by the Government via a quasi-public company to minimise their apparent borrowing for Treasury accounting reasons. The Labour Government, which wants to reduce the present subsidies, seems uncertain about how to tackle the basic problem of an unsatisfactory form of privatisation, whilst the Conservatives have yet to reveal their proposals.

Nevertheless the basic problems remain, for even the Rail Regulator, Bill Emery, recently remarked that 'British Railways has been splintered into over one hundred separate companies, each with its own set of lawyers contesting its rights'. Indeed, a number of vital track upgrades, including those to the West Coast Main Line, have suffered long overruns, causing major disruption to passengers at critical times.

Metronet won the PPP contract to modernise the TfL sub-surface lines and embarked on an upgrade of the Met and associated railways. Here at Amersham one of the GBRf class 66s that they leased is positioning ballast wagons. Some of these diesels were given names relevant to the Joint, such as *Sir Edward Watkin*, *Metro-land* and above, *Valour*. This was the nameplate carried by the GCR First World War Remembrance locomotive. (*C.A.F. Coll*)

The financial crisis of 2008, which has further restricted the funds available to Network Rail and also equity investment, is placing new strains on the present model of privatisation. It has altered the whole basis of existing investments, such as the value of the TOC franchises and the trains owned by the leasing companies. It also highlights another of the 'Unintended Consequences' of this form of privatisation, namely that in the open competition to participate, overseas companies have attained a substantial position as TOCs and suppliers. These are usually global players who are prepared to buy their way into the UK market, but who are not necessarily subservient to the wishes of the UK Government and tend to act in relation to the world situation, which can create major problems.

As it happens, this last aspect relates to the operators that now use the old Joint Lines. The presentiment of Chris Green in forming the Chiltern Line as a separate concern with modern equipment had inevitably made it a prime candidate for privatisation, and in 1996 a group of investors, led by John Laing, won a seven year franchise to run it as a private company – M40 Trains, or Chiltern Railways. With Adrian Shooter still at the helm, new developments included more trains, of both the Type 165 Turbos and also the improved Type 168 Clubmans, more suited to the longer distance routes that were being re-introduced on the old GW&GC Joint Line to Birmingham and beyond. As a result, in 2003 it was not only the expansion of their services but also their reliability which enabled Chiltern Railways to win the competition for the next franchise, giving them an exceptional twenty-year extension.

Since that point, the many new undertakings have been fully implemented. In the case of infrastructure, double-track that had been removed as a consequence of 'Beeching' has been replaced on the Birmingham line, providing a very competitive alternative to the route from Euston, and the line has now been extended to Kidderminster. More stations have been upgraded, including Marylebone, where two new platforms have been added with space having been freed by building a new re-fuelling/stock depot at Wembley. With the addition of more Type 168 Clubmans the effective capacity of Chiltern Railways has been increased by more than 50 per cent, and the customers are being encouraged to utilise this through a range of services including innovative online information, ticketing facilities and secure convenient parking.

So, in 2006 all seemed to be set fair for the future of Chiltern Railways when their parent company, Laing, was suddenly bought by Henderson, a fund management company, with the objective of realising the undervalued assets of their railway activities. Apart from Chiltern Railways, these also included a share in London Overground (the old North London Railway being revitalised by the successor to LT, Transport for London, or TfL), and a stake in a new TOC, the Wrexham & Shropshire Railway. This was created in May 2008 and started to operate services from Marylebone to that area via Banbury and Wolverhampton. Initially these services are being operated with some three coaches, top and tailed by EWS type 67s diesel locomotives to avoid having to run round at the end of the journey.

An interior view of the new Bombardier S8 (sub surface-eight coach) stock for use on the Met. It shows open layout with the ability to walk between coaches, easier wheelchair access and increase in standing room capacity. Delivery is now due in 2012. (*C.A.F. Coll*)

Chiltern Railways have their chief maintenance Depot at just north of Aylesbury. The three modern Chiltern DMUs in the picture are the more recent Type 168 Clubman Turbostars and the ex-BR DMU is one of several refurbished at the Depot. This example is used for track testing whilst another provides a shuttle service to Princes Risborough. (*C.A.F. Coll*)

However, the subsequent auction by Henderson's was won by Deutsche Bahn, the German railway operator who had also recently acquired Britain's largest freight train railway company, the English, Welsh & Scottish Railways, which had been formed from the privatisation of BR. Paradoxically, Laing appeared to wish to sell Chiltern Railways, a growing and successful company, because it was more advantageous to do so whilst there were about fifteen more years of their franchise left to run.

Conversely, Deutsche Bahn bought the railway assets of Laing as part of a long-term strategy of expansion in the UK. Whilst the size and ambitions of Deutsche Bahn should indicate that it will be taking a positive and long-term view of its investments in the UK, it is itself currently undergoing considerable change. Deutsche Bahn, or the 'Bahn' as it is known in Germany, is a nationalised body, having been formed with the unification of the country, and is now being prepared for semi-privatisation. Its existing operations, which were losing some €10 billion per annum, have been streamlined, with the workforce being halved to 250,000 and with a loss of €313 billion turned into a profit of €1.7 billion.

On the basis of intentions to transform the company into a worldwide logistics operation, some 25 per cent of the new company is to be floated on the stock exchange. Apparently they hope to avoid the 'disadvantages' of the UK rail privatisation by retaining ownership of both the rail operations and the infrastructure in the state-owned holding company, Deutsche Bahn AG, via two subsidiaries. One will be responsible for the infrastructure, and the other, DB Mobility Logistics AG, will run all the services, including those in the UK.

Within this, the former EWS freight business has been renamed DB Schenker. It is the DB Mobility Logistics operation that is due to be privatised, with the aim of selling some 49.9 per cent of the company. It has the objective of further expansion of their presence in the UK and elsewhere, and indeed, late in 2008 it took the opportunity of the weakness in the UK economy to acquire Porterbrook Holdings for some £2 billion. As this company leased a significant amount of rolling stock to the other TOCs, this again increased the influence of Deutsche Bahn in this country.

In addition, Deutsche Bahn is negotiating with Eurotunnel for its own dedicated high-speed paths for services to the Continent. All this will give Deutsche Bahn a significant presence in the UK and could influence the future direction of Chiltern Railways, who are already extending services to the Welsh Borders. They have also obtained a seven-year franchise extension to upgrade the Birmingham route and create a line to Oxford. This suggests that Deutsche Bahn intend to be a major railway operator in the UK.

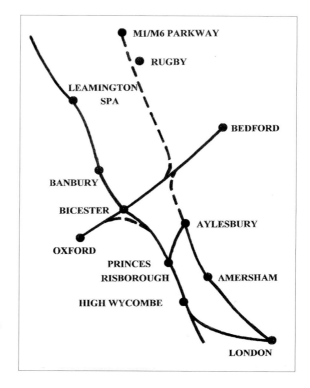

Although many plans have been made to re-open the Met & GC lines north of Aylesbury, little Government action has resulted. Nevertheless, in small increments Chiltern Railways have steadily revitalised the prospects and this schematic map shows their objectives under the new umbrella of D Bahn. (C.A.F. Coll)

In parallel with this turmoil over the implementation of the privatisation of BR, the Labour government favoured a somewhat different approach for privatising the rail operations of London Transport (LUL), by means of their then preferred mechanism of the Public private partnership (PPP). In this arrangement, private companies can build and operate a service – such as a hospital or railway – at an agreed cost, on behalf of the Government for the benefit of the public. London Underground Ltd recognised that something like this was now inevitable, and to ease such a transition they divided their rail operations as far as possible into 'TOC-like' separate units.

Thus, in 2001 the Metropolitan and associated sub-surface lines were given their own shadow management, with limited powers to prepare for the PPP era. This interregnum produced some significant improvements in service via better deployment of their resources. Also, recognising that there was little likelihood of soon replacing the ageing A60/2 stock working the Met Line, a complete refurbishment was undertaken between 1994–7, which included a graffiti-resistant outer finish and the addition of end windows to the coaches for better visibility in order to reduce anti-social behaviour. However, the maximum speed of Metropolitan trains remained at 50mph.

Meanwhile, in 2003 the Government started the PPP bidding process for the LUL railways in two parts: the 'deep tube lines', and the predominately 'sub-surface lines'. The latter group included the Met, District, Circle and Hammersmith routes, as well as the Bakerloo, Central, Victoria and the Waterloo & City tubes. However, the Government – which had created the new post of Mayor of London with responsibility for inner London (including its transport) – was somewhat surprised when their candidate was beaten by the Labour maverick Ken Livingstone. On taking office in 2000, he immediately took a special interest in transport, bringing it together as Transport for London (TfL) and opposing the privatisation of LUL railways, and in particular the PPP method.

His opposition was based on the expense and unclear responsibilities and he fought hard against it, in the end taking it to the High Court where he eventually lost the case. In parallel, the bidding for the two PPP operations dragged on, with significant concessions being obtained by the contractors until, in 2002, the Metronet consortium won a thirty-year franchise to maintain and improve the Met and other sub-surface lines, reporting to TfL. The 'deep tube' PPP was awarded to the Tube Lines consortium.

As described earlier, TfL inherited both an ageing infrastructure and trains, so Metronet began to implement an agreed programme to replace the relevant rolling stock with a common design of sub-surface stock, to renew the track and signalling, and to modernise the stations. Inevitably, the five member companies of the Metronet consortium expected to – and did – benefit from the work undertaken. Certainly the proposals tackled not only the fundamental issues of replacing the infrastructure, but also a radical review of operating schedules and practices in order to improve efficiency of the network in terms of cost and services.

It is perhaps indicative of the complexity of the contractual relationships that the legal fees amounted to some £500 million before work actually started. Orders were eventually placed with Bombardier for new common stock to replace the old LT A60/2, C and

Above left: The decision to build some 15,000 new houses on the outskirts of Aylesbury provided the impetus to reopen the Joint to a new station on the A41 a few miles north of the present station. Opened in December 2008 as Aylesbury Vale Parkway forming a hub for other transport, it provides a frequent service to Aylesbury and Marylebone. (*Roger Marks*)

Above right: Currently, twice a day, a large train of London refuse travels out via Aylesbury to a landfill site at Calvert on the old GC line. Here asuch a DB Shenker train headed by an ex-EWS Class 66 diesel No. 66110 is approaching the new Aylesbury Vale Station. (*Roger Marks*)

D stock. A massive programme of track replacement started, which involved leasing some six GBRF type 66 diesel locomotives and complementary relaying wagons, re-signalling contracts using Westinghouse, and refurbishing all stations.

However, as the work progressed there was increasing unhappiness on the part of both Metronet and TfL over the slipping timescales and escalating costs. Ken Livingstone blamed the contractors for poor project management and undoubtedly felt that this justified his earlier opposition to the PPP approach that had been forced on him by the Government. Metronet however claimed that TfL had underestimated the amount of work that would be needed, and that they continually changed their requirements.

These difficulties escalated during 2006–7, until Metronet was placed in administration as a result of an overrun on the contract of some £2 billion, which TfL refused to pay. This disagreement was sent for arbitration. It was decided that both parties were equally to blame, but the side 'letters of comfort' given to the Metronet partners by the Government limited their liability to some £70 million each. Following this settlement the administrators were able to take Metronet out of insolvency, and its activities and staffs were transferred to TfL on 27 May 2008.

The latest indications from TfL are that the majority of existing contracts will be continuing, such as the new sub-surface trains from Bombardier, although some issues are being re-visited, including the phasing of the introduction of the longer S8 version of the trains for the Met. The original plan was that the first of these would be deployed on the Met, followed by the seven-car S7s on the Circle, Hammersmith & City and District lines, but there are problems in accommodating the S7s at some of the stations such as Hammersmith and Edgware Road.

As an interim solution, it was proposed that first the Hammersmith & City lines will use the six-car S6s prior to the Olympics, with a business case created for the necessary infrastructure improvements to accommodate the S7s after the Olympics. While the Met should have had the first of the new trains, now the S6s will be built first as a priority for the Hammersmith & City line to serve East London for the Olympics, followed by the S7s and S8s. So *Metro-land* will have to wait until around 2012 for the new services.

As the design of the new S8 stock did not allow the separation into four-car operation, this implied the end of the Chesham Shuttle service. Without admitting this, in 2008 TfL undertook a pseudo public consultation on replacing the Shuttle with two through trains to London per hour, which would result in the reduction of their trains from Amersham from four to two per hour – albeit still having the excellent Chiltern Railways service. In view of the traditionally strong objections from the Amersham commuters, it was somewhat surprising that TfL declared that the vote supported the new proposals, and so, after over seventy years, Frank Pick and LT are at last getting rid of the anomalous Chesham Shuttle! Indeed, as a further blow, it seems as if the extra trains from Chesham may run to Watford.

However, even then *Metro-landers* may find that this new stock takes some getting used to. Certainly there will be the advantages of air conditioning, and a 'bendy bus' construction will give easier access between coaches as well as facilities for the disabled. However, the seating will be more basic and its capacity reduced to cope with the number of standing passengers on the Inner Circle section of the Met route.

Some of the contracts are being re-tendered under TfL procurement rules, such as the re-signalling work by Westinghouse, whose automatic train control system was found to be incompatible with that of Thales which is being installed on Tube lines. In addition, new contracts have already been placed for rebuilding Neasden Depot to house and service most of the fleet of new trains for all the sub-service lines. This will involve replacing some 80 per cent of the existing depot. The contract for replacing the relevant signalling at Neasden has now been placed with Thales.

There are examples of successful PPP projects in other fields, but Tubelines, the other TfL PPP contractor for the deep tubes, is apparently encountering problems. In practice, with many PPP schemes, problems have been found to lie in differences between the parties in the interpretation of the contracts and in controlling any changes to it. In the case of Metronet, these issues seem to have been compounded by the nature of their consortium, unclear responsibilities and failures in project control. On the TfL side, as situations change there must have been the natural tendency for 'specification drift', the temptation to modify plans and to add improvements – all of which result in delays and extra cost.

It now remains to be seen how the new arrangement will work with Metronet's activities back in the public domain within TfL. Particularly because of another surprising shift of power, Ken Livingstone, who had come to be tolerated by the Labour government, was ousted by Conservative Boris Johnson as Mayor of London in 2008. As described earlier, most of Metronet's original plans seem to be being carried forward, but undoubtedly some things will change as a result of union reactions to the need to shed the extra staff that had been recruited to manage Metronet and the current financial stringencies.

CHAPTER EIGHT

THE FUTURE, AND BACK AGAIN

LIKELY DEVELOPMENTS

In retrospect, Beeching's cuts of 1963 now seem to be yet another example of the 'Law of Unintended Consequences', in that the emphasis has since changed to reflect pressing concerns with energy and the environment, in which railways can have significant advantages over pervasive motor vehicles. The effect of the Beeching closures was fundamentally to weaken the roots of the network, thereby making access more difficult, and then, by slimming down the trunk network, drastically reducing the capacity and resilience that is currently so needed by Network Rail.

However, that period of retrenchment caused a fundamental shift in customer attitude. Whereas at one time a station existed in virtually every small town, and every factory had its own siding, now most people and most companies have to use motor vehicles to reach the nearest railway, and so, for convenience, why not for the rest of the journey? It is difficult to conceive how this opinion can be completely reversed without that extensive infrastructure of the past. Nevertheless, the relative improvement in rail services in comparison with growing congestion on the roads has encouraged a resurgence in railway passenger traffic over the past decade of 40 per cent, so that currently more people are using the railways than since the last war.

Equally, for heavy freight the growth has continued at a rate of 50 per cent over a decade, and with growing demand there is an urgent need to increase this capacity. In view of the relatively small amount that can be added to the existing capacity by removing bottlenecks, in 2008 Network Rail initiated a study of building a series of new high-speed lines for fast traffic adjacent to existing routes. One of these is to be the Chiltern Railways route from Marylebone to the Midlands: Watkin would be turning in his grave if it were not the third such report in recent years, and in any case there is little likelihood of any investment of this scale being made available. The reality is that since 2002 the Government expenditure on roads has risen by some 60 per cent, whilst that on railways has risen by less than 10 per cent, and even then crucial bottlenecks cannot be eased for lack of funding.

There have been many grandiose schemes for new trunk railways in recent years that could have impacted on the Met & GC Joint Lines, but all have faded away. However, there are some other relevant proposals that are still pending. Of these, CrossRail, at one time, would have dramatically changed the role of the Met. It was conceived by LT in the

1960s as a 4-mile-long, 6-metre-diameter large-bore deep tube between Paddington and Liverpool Street to ease cross-London traffic. This core aspect has remained constant over subsequent years, but the extent of the surface extensions at either end have altered to reflect changing political priorities and the need to attract more traffic to justify the high costs involved. With such longer routes, longer trains and higher speeds, the line will now use a 25kv overhead electric system.

To the east, an extension would have originally gone to Shenfield via Stratford, and this was reinforced by the decision to locate the 2012 Olympic Games nearby, with the ability for passengers to join Eurostar trains. However, in addition there will now be a branch to Abbey Wood to serve the rapidly developing Docklands area. To the west, the proposed extension to Reading now includes a branch to the airport at Heathrow. Yet it was to the north-west of London that the planned route would have had a dramatic effect on the Met and Chiltern Railways, for a branch of CrossRail was intended to leave the main line from Paddington, near Old Oak Common, and turn northwards to join the Chiltern Railways line at Neasden to run on to Aylesbury.

Inevitably this would have affected both LT as well as Chiltern Railways, albeit in different ways. For Chiltern there was the short-term frustration that this route would stop them building their new servicing depot at Neasden. More fundamentally, it would have altered the basis of their operating franchise. In contrast, for LT it would have completed Pick's plans and rid them of most of the anomalous vestiges of the Met. This was because, with CrossRail serving Rickmansworth and the stations to Chesham and Aylesbury, LT routes could then have been retrenched to Watford and Uxbridge.

As time has passed, the cost has inevitably escalated and financing has become more difficult, so these plans have been gradually truncated to the point where the CrossRail route to Aylesbury was abandoned in 2008. Even so, the estimated £16 billion for financing CrossRail remains the main problem in that it is now a fully owned subsidiary of TfL, albeit with support from the British Airports Authority, the City of London via business rates, a Canary Wharf consortium and also the Government.

An Enabling Act of 2008 allowed the main construction to start in two years time, but necessary work arising from other overlapping TfL projects, such as at Canary Wharf, started in May 2009. However, serious objections are still being made, particularly by the rail freight lobby, who believe that their existing train paths will be restricted, and by landowners against the compulsory purchase orders. In addition, the dire economic situation has impacted on the search for funding, and in particular on the hope that legislation will be passed to enable the business rates of the area to be increased to reflect the enhanced future value of the properties. The first trains might run in 2017 – too late for the Olympics.

Meanwhile, against the background of this scheme – which is incurring annual costs of about £100 million (even whilst it is not being built!) just for planning and 'safeguarding' the route – there are much more modest proposals that offer a disproportionately larger improvement in railway services relevant to this story. One such long-standing proposal very relevant to the Met is the Watford Link, of less than three miles long and connecting the Watford Met line to the West Coast Main Line via the disused BR branch to Croxley. This very useful project has much support from all parties, but as the cost has tripled over the past ten years to some £145 million, it is likely to remain in limbo during the recession.

Whilst there have also been many suggestions for re-opening Watkin's London Extension to provide more capacity, none have yet survived. However, there are a few activities on the moribund route of the old Met & GC Joint Line that might come together to re-open this section. Fortunately, since closure this track has remained singled in order to give refuse trains from London access to the landfill site at Calvert Brickworks. It has also been used by some special trains as well as DMUs to take visitors to the flourishing Buckinghamshire Railway Centre, based at the refurbished Quainton Road Station, albeit restricted to a speed limit of 15mph.

More recently, as part of the Government's intention to build more housing in Buckinghamshire, there will be a major development of over 15,000 new houses at Berryfields, adjacent to the A41 some 3 miles north of Aylesbury. As part of this scheme the Government, Buckinghamshire County, local Council and Chiltern Railways have together given £8 million to upgrade the track and build a new station adjacent to this site. This Aylesbury Vale Parkway Station was opened ahead of schedule in December 2008, offering parking for 400 cars and with a service of two trains per hour to Marylebone at peak times, and one train at other times.

The related initiative that would encourage use of the northern Met & GC Joint Line, via access at Claydon Junction, is that of the East-West Rail Consortium. Launched in 1999, this project would re-open and upgrade the old Varsity Line between Oxford and Cambridge. This could provide a much needed cross-country rail link from the east coast ports which would avoid the necessity of travelling in to London and out again, thus taking pressure off the overloaded radial routes. It would only involve upgrading/ restoring the tracks between Bicester and Bletchley, as well as Bletchley to Cambridge, although some houses have been built across the tracks!

After years of government prevarication some of the interested parties seem to have taken matters into their own hands. The Milton Keynes Partnership has contracted WS Atkins to clear the overgrowth from the Newton Longville and Claydon section of the route, and, in the rebuilding of Milton Keynes Station, facilities have been provided for any trains from the re-opened East-West Link. More recently, use of part of the Varsity Line has been proposed by Chiltern Railways, with a £220 million investment for running a service from Marylebone to Oxford via a new quarter-mile link from their line at Bicester. Work is expected to begin in 2011 and this would offer a sixty-six-minute journey time to Oxford as well as greatly strengthening the case for a complete re-opening of the east-west route.

However, seeing that the Government seems unable to fund even the construction of the vital easement of existing railway bottlenecks – that would undoubtedly give a dramatic improvement – apart from the proposal of Chiltern Railways, it is problematic to support any of the above, let alone new, high-speed lines.

CHAPTER NINE

'IN REMEMBRANCE OF THINGS PAST'

During the 1950s it became apparent that the Met steam locomotives, retained in 1937 by LT for works and engineering use, were becoming uneconomic to maintain. However, there was still need for motive power that did not depend on electricity, and so consideration was given to acquiring some surplus steam and diesel locomotives from BR. None of the types on offer were suitable, but it was recalled that some ex-GWR pannier tank locomotives had success-fully assisted LT during the post-war construction of the Extension to the Central Line.

After trials, some eleven of the 77xx 0-6-0 pannier tank engines were transferred to the Met between 1956 and 1963 to replace the remaining Met E, F and Peckett tank engines. These became a familiar sight on the Met: shunting, hauling permanent way trains, the Cowans Sheldon breakdown train and the daily trips to the dump near the Watford triangle. However, by the end of the 1950s even these panniers were reaching the end of their useful lives. To mark the end of over 100 years of steam haulage on the Met a 'Farewell to Steam' event was held on 6 June 1971, during which maroon pannier No.L94 took a train of LT's engineering rolling stock from Moorgate, through the origi-nal Met tunnels to emerge at Finchley Road, and on to an exhibition at Neasden Depot.

It was poignant reminder that it was a Great Western locomotive that was called upon to haul the first public trains over the Met, and now it was another that would produce the last unforgettable sights, sounds and smells of a steam train thundering through the tunnels and brick chasms of the Met. The sight of their exhausts rising through the grat-ings down the centre of the Euston Road would not be repeated.

Later, the centenary of the opening of the Chesham branch was celebrated in fine style in 1989, when the management of the Met collaborated with Chesham Town Council and others in running a vintage shuttle to Chalfont & Latimer and then returning from Watford. One of the steam locomotives was the original E1 class 'Met 1', which had just been restored by the Bucks Railway Centre, and the train was appropriately tailed by the remaining Bo–Bo electric locomotive, *Sarah Siddons*. This inaugurated some 11 years of 'Steam on the Met' with a variety of engines, many of which had worked the Met during its heyday. Unfortunately, more stringent health and safety regulations, combined with a less enthusiastic management regime, brought the events to a sad end.

However, 'Steam on the Met' did recharge nostalgic memories for many of those who had known the real Met. The sight of elegant rolling stock (fit for purpose), the characteristic sounds of both steam and Bo–Bo electric locomotives, even the smells of smoke, leather and moquette,

The classic image of the Met Shuttle from Chesham having breasted the 1 in 66 climb from the Chess Valley, rounding Raans Farm for the approach to Chalfont & Latimer Station. Enthusiastic drivers used to race the mainline train to reach the station first. (*Photomatic*)

A C13 engine simmers gently in the background during a formal inspection of Chesham Station on the 15 March 1953. From the left are Alrex Webb (General Superintendent), Colonel Gordon Maxwell of Ardwell (Operating Manager, Railways with traditional trilby), A.B.Valentine (Chairman) and the station master, Henry 'John' Hudson with the obligatory flower in his buttonhole. (*Jean Catherine*)

and brake dust. Nevertheless, even the most ardent advocate of the Met would reluctantly be forced to admit that these would be incompatible with the demands of the present day. Even so, it was the manner in which the Met and its staff used the equipment that it had available that was crucial to creating the esteem in which it was held. This sentiment was encapsulated in a recent speech by Adrian Shooter, Chairman of the very successful Chiltern Railways:

…the Metropolitan Railway of years gone by knew what the public wanted – reliable clean trains, good information regarding services, a seat, value for money and easy ticketing – and that is the same today.

However, the railway system evolves over the next few years, those involved in shaping it should remember well these lessons demonstrated by the Metropolitan Railway. Inevitably it will be impossible to recapture the feeling of something special when travelling on the Met. It was a longer experience with a certain irrevocability about it – so vastly different from a trip on the London Underground, where you could change your mind and recover your position within a few minutes of leaving. Instead it was the sensation of release, of being able to leave the crowds and bustle of London behind to embark on a *real* journey. So, in order to recall those experiences, this book ends with some pictures creating a vignette of that classic Met experience – the Chesham Shuttle.

With electrification, and the removal of the original Met water crane at the end of the Chesham platform, an ex-GWR water tower had been installed near the signal box. Here, on the last day of steam haulage, still wreathed with laurels, BR No. 41284 has its side tanks replenished. (*Ron White*)

Travelling on the Met – once upon a time! (*C.A.F. Coll*)

APPENDIX I

FINANCIAL PERFORMANCE

The fortunes of the railways that this book is concerned with involve the Metropolitan – a commuter line, the Great Central – a national mainline, and their Joint Line – reluctantly created out of necessity. Their financial inheritance of the machinations of Sir Edward Watkin was to dominate their performance, and as a result the opinions of historians have differed strongly over their respective viability and commercial success.

In a sense, the Joint was a free-standing company, and thus presented its own accounts. Incomes from passenger and goods traffic, as well as that from rental (land, buildings and commercial sites), were set by a broad competitive environment On the other hand, costs were related to labour and infrastructure investment plus financial overheads. In this respect the owners of the Joint were not well placed, having inherited the aftermath of the high costs of their construction.

The MS&LR route had dramatically exceeded the budget and delayed income, to be later compounded by the costs of Watkin's London Extension. In contrast, its partner, the Met, was initially inundated with passengers but suffered from financial malpractice before Watkin arrived. Although his battles with James Staats Forbes and the construction of the Extension were expensive, he managed to pay moderate dividends helped by the income from property and other holdings. Afterwards, the reign of Selbie was characterised by lower dividends as a result of the cost of electrification and factors common to all railways, such as the First War, the General Strike and increasing competition from motor vehicles.

It was common practice in the Victorian era to pay dividends during the construction phase. Both companies had 'avoided the evil day' by continuing to raise fresh finance – whilst paying dividends out of their existing capital – to try and keep the shareholders happy. This was made possible by the issuing of preference shares and debentures as bait. Although this imprudent approach was not uncommon, it was its scale that in the longer term added to their ongoing financial burden. When Watkin arrived on the railway scene he created a financial smokescreen, and then made it worse by embarking on his massive investment to bring about his vision.

From our present perspective it is difficult to judge the viability of the Met and the GCR as owners of the Joint, whose financial positions had ramifications for that company. The accounting conventions of the Victorian and Edwardian era were different and more lax than our own, and items such as the treatment of depreciation, work in progress and the allocation of overheads were susceptible to 'creative accounting'. Equally, the evaluation of what classifies as a 'good' or a 'bad' performance changes over time, with varying emphasis on growth, dividend income and potential. Overlaying this assessment is the 'sentiment' of the stock market towards a particular sector, which in this case was known as 'Home Rails'. During the early years, optimism drove shares to unsustainable levels until the bubble burst around 1849, and then, as railways matured, their stock became a safe blue-chip investment for many. However, as railway competition increased and road transport developed, 'Home Rails' steadily declined. The sad fortunes of the MS&LR and its successor the GCR were parodied at the time as 'Money Sunk & Lost' and 'Gone Completely', however, more recent studies have presented a more considered assessment.

On the one hand, Messrs Emblin, Longbone & Jackson point out that the inevitably costly expansion of the Met and GWR London Extensions, as well as the improved facilities on the East-West coast route, were essential to the survival, profit and growth of the GCR. Although these created a debt which had to be serviced, it was not true that the GCR never paid a dividend. Indeed, the majority of shares were non-contingent and dividends were paid on most of these. After Watkin, the excellent management team led by Henderson exploited the earlier massive investment, and the authors point out that although the finances of the GCR were never robust, they were not greatly dissimilar to the rest of the 'Home Rails'. Equally, when 'grouping' was inevitable in 1923, the GCR became a valued constituent of the LNER.

By contrast, Messrs Bloxsom & Hendry trace the origins of the problems of GCR to the ongoing crippling debt incurred by the Sheffield, Ashton-under-Lyne & Manchester Railway, exacerbated by the later schemes of the MS&LR and the GCR. The consequent capital structure of the companies drained profits into the preference dividends, leaving an inherent financial weakness that led to merger negotiations in the early 1900s. 'Grouping' overtook these, and in the resulting LNER the fragility of the GCR was counterbalanced by the more prosperous NER.

The 'truth' probably lies somewhere between these two viewpoints, but from our current interest in the Joint the essential factor is that the debt/dividend considerations meant that any transfer charges were loaded and GCR investment was not a priority in – what they saw as – a Met commuter line. Equally, the Met under Seblie had to 'run a tight ship,' to the extent that LT complained that the Met infrastructure was inferior to their own network. This all led to a prudent culture in the Joint, in which all expenditure was carefully vetted and where the partners were suspicious of any spend favouring the operations of the other party.

Against this background it is appropriate to turn to the reported financial performance of the Joint. In the following table – which has been constructed from available accounts – the headings have been recast in an attempt to produce comparable figures. These have been rounded to the nearest £, therefore there may be some small inconsistencies. Nevertheless it shows some interesting features and trends in passenger and goods traffic. In 1913 the net revenue was split between the Met & the GCR, but, as a result of nego-tiation, the accounts for 1923 onward show a preferential profit of £5,000 for the Met before the sharing.

The financial significance of Joint to the respective partners can be crudely shown by comparing a typi-cal profit for each from the Joint in the early 1920s of about £40,000 with the overall profit of the GCR of around £2 million and the Met some £800,000. However, the transit traffic was more valuable to both.

MET & GC JT. COMMITTEE REVENUE ACCOUNTS (£)

YEAR	1913	1922	1924	1925	1936	1937
RECEIPTS						
Passenger						
First	7,829	16,261	174,161	162,682	7,012	7,999
Third	75,948	101,475	(inc third)	(inc third)	113,047	118,343
Season	13,755	48,445	52,042	52,350	68,113	71,673
Workmen	294	715	867	1,191	6.603	6,948
Parcels/mail	40,092	57,281	57,165	61,410	72,459	61,663
Total	**137,920**	**281,177**	**284,235**	**277,633**	**267,234**	**266,619**
Goods						
Merchandise([2])	24,683	47,622	27,023	32,573	23,364	24,800
Livestock	1,000	2,036	1,610	2,360	844	83
Coal etc.	19,814	33,914	40,242	38,462	41,362	41,012
Other minerals	10,140	22,102	35,204	31,612	15,510	8,776
Misc.	870	2,659	1,821	1,742	3,921	5,022
Total op. revenue	**56,508**	**108,334**	**105,900**	**106,749**	**83,627**	**79,693**
Rents & other Receipts	7,061	10,446	13,187	13,077	14,171	13,819
TOTAL	**210,490**	**399,957**	**403,322**	**397,459**	**366,406**	**360,131**
EXPENDITURE						
Permanent way	31,813	80,153	71,761	63,782	63771	64,449
Shunting loco exp.	2,812	11,667	12,701	11,933	8,971	9,971
Traffic expenses	20,108	62,286	58,445	60,882	([o])58,243	59,485
Legal/rent etc.	7,249	4,877	13,857	13,677	15,638	15,316
Running powers	58,643	120,684	117,738	([1])112,898	110,628	113,431
Misc.	27	117	115	110	–	–
Total op. exp.	**120,652**	**289,784**	**274,617**	**263,282**	**257,211**	**262,652**
Interest, rentals & fixed charges([3])	51,734	51,735	46,237	46,237	45,723	45,635
TOTAL	**172,386**	**341,519**	**320,854**	**309,519**	**302,934**	**308,287**
NET REVENUE TO SHARE	**29,104**	**29,219**	**82,468**	**87,940**	**63,472**	**51,844**

Notes:
(o) including salaries of £42,275
(1) passenger: Met = £34,353 + LNER = £55,823
   goods: Met = £19,252 + LNER = £3,420
(2) net of delivery costs
(3) including rent of leased lines, i.e. Met & GC Joint = £44,000 + OAT = £600

The above figures include the reported profit/loss for the Watford branch, which in:

1936	−£8,659	1937	−£7,612	1938	−£7,467
1939	−£10,465	1940	£51,099	1941	£73,157
1942	£32,916	1943	£57,512	1944	£36,897
1945	£41,861	1946	£43,028	1947	£39,176

APPENDIX 2

'JOINT' STATISTICS

TRACK LENGTH

Overall length of Joint = 48.5 miles, including Chesham branch (4 miles), Watford branch (2 miles 37 chains) and the moiety of Aylesbury Joint Station.

STAFF NUMBERS

In 1906 – 181
In 1947 – 396

FARES

1914	1d per mile
1917	1.5d: to discourage wartime travel
1920	1.75d
1923	1.5d: upon grouping
1937	1.575d
1947	2.5d: post-war

TRAFFIC IN 1925

Engine Mileage

Steam:

Coaching:	Met	322,581
	LNE	588,674
Goods	Met	149,620
	LNE	19,746
Electric:	Met	224,300
Total miles		**1,304,951**

Passenger Numbers

Originating on Joint	3,512,993
Total	**13,016,999**

Goods

	Originating on Joint	Total
Merchandise	15,370	140,772
Coal, etc.	756	328,440

Other minerals	63,162	285,220
Total tons	79,288	754,432
Livestock numbers	27,177	40,172

STATIONS

Name	Opened	Changes
Harrow on the Hill	2 Aug. 1880	–
North Harow Halt	22 Mar. 1915	North Harrow 1928
Pinner	1 May. 1885	–
Northwood Hills	13 Nov. 1933	–
Northwood	1 Sept. 1887	–
Sandy Lodge	9 Apr. 1910	Moor Park & Sandy Lodge 18 Oct. 1923; Moor Park 1958
Croxley Green	2 Nov. 1925	–
Watford	2 Nov. 1925	–
Rickmansworth	1 Sept. 1887	–
Chorley Wood	8 Jul. 1889	Chorley Road 1889?; Chorley Wood & Chenies 1915; Chorley Wood 1958; Chorleywood 1961
Chalfont Road	8 Jul. 1889	Chalfont & Latimer 20 Nov. 1915
Chesham	8 Jul. 1889	–
Amersham	1 Sept. 1892	Amersham 1920; Amersham & Chesham Bois 1922; Amersham 1939
Great Missenden	1 Sept. 1892	–
Wendover	1 Sept. 1892	–
Stoke Mandeville	1 Sept. 1892	–
Aylesbury (Town)	GWR 20 Oct. 1863	–
	OAT 23 Sept. 1868	–
	Met 1 Sept.1892	–
Waddesdon Manor	1 Jan. 1897	Waddesdon 1 Oct. 1922; Closed 6 Jul. 1936
Quainton Road	23 Sept. 1868	Closed Met pass 29 May. 1948; Closed BR pass 4 Mar. 1963; goods Jul. 1966
Waddesdon	1 Apr. 1871	Waddesdon Road 1 Oct. 1922; Closed 30 Nov. 1935
Wescott	1 Apr. 1871	Closed 30 Nov. 1935
Woods Siding	1 Apr, 1871	Closed 30 Nov. 1935
Brill	Mar. 1872	Closed 30 Nov. 1935
Grandborough Road	23 Sept. 1868	Granborough Road 6 Oct. 1920; Closed pass. 4 Jul. 1936
Winslow Road	23 Sept. 1868	Closed pass. 4 Jul. 1936
Verney Junction (Met)	23 Sept. 1868	Closed pass. 4 Jul. 1936; goods 6 Sept. 1947

MILEPOSTS

GCR/LNER: located on the up side, from zero at Manchester (London Road). Met/LT: from Harrow to Quainton Road, downside, from zero at Baker Street. 'South' refers to south of mp 28.5 etc.

GOODS SERVICES: 1931 WEEKDAYS

a) LNER

Down: MB (02.50) – HH (03.27)   Up: HH (04.25) – Neasden,LNER
       QR (11.55) – WD   WD (03.00) – QR (04.04)
       QR (20.10) – WD   HH (23.40) – MB
       MB (22.15) – HH (22.32)   WD (03.25) – QR (07.16)

b) Met

(excluding various shunting, elec. loco movements south of Neasden & Chesham branch goods with 'Shuttle'. Some trains called at any station as requested.)

Train No.

1	down	FR (03.45)-HH -C&L-all to QR-VJ (14.00)
	up	VJ (15.50)-QR-AYL-WR-GM-C&L-RW-all-HH-WG-Neasden (02.18)
2	down	FR (05.25)-HH-PN-RW-all to VJ (19.02)
	up	VJ (08.25)-QR-GM-HH-Neasden,Met (12.31)
2a	down	ND (04.30)-HH-WAT-RW (06.14)
3	down	FR (21.17)-WG-ND-HH-RW-C&L-AYL-QR-VJ (06.10)
	up	VJ (08.10)-all to C&L-RW-WAT-PN-HH-Neasden,Met (23.08)
4	down	ND (19.30)-HH-AYL-QR (22.15)
	up	QR (23.25)-AYL-HH-Neasden,Met (03.15)
5	down	ND (01.05)-AYL-QR (03.45)
	up	QR (05.)-AYL-RW-WAT-NW-HH-WP-ND (12.23)
6	down	Light engine & brake van: ND (Met) (03.10)-HH-WE-AYL (05.07)
	up	VJ (00.10)-QR-(00.55) to BRILL
	up	VJ (13.50)-AYL-RW-HH-WP-Neasden,Met (15.10)
8	down	ND (05.10)-HH-HILL-UX (06.43)
	up	UX (08.42)-RP-RL-HH (10.49)
	down	HH (10.59)-GWS (11.10)
	up	GWS (11.33)-HH-WP-ND-WG- Neasden,Met (14.41)
10	down	ND (07.38)-HH-NW-WSJ-RW-C&L-CH (14.22)
	up	CH (16.25)-ND (17.19)
11	down	FR (06.50)-WG(shunt yard)-Neasden,Met (10.37)
12	down	ND (03.25)-HH-WE-AYL (05.07)
	up	AYL (01.50)-C&L-HH-Neasden,Met (03.50)
15	down	Light engine & brake van: ND (Met)(10.34)-VJ (12.21)
	up	VJ (13.50)-AYL-RW-ND (17.06)

Key: AYL: Aylesbury; C&L: Chalfont & Latimer; CH: Chesham; CW: Chorley Wood; FR: Finchley Road; GSW: Gas Works siding (S.Harrow); HILL: Hillingdon; HH: Harrow; ND: Neasden; NW: Northwood; PN: Pinner; QR: Quainton Rd.; RW: Rickm'th; SM: Stoke Mandeville; RL: Rayners Lane; RP: Ruislip; UX: Uxbridge; VJ: Verney Junction; WAT: Watford; WD: Woodford; WE: Wendover; WG: Willesden Green; WP: Wembley Park; WSJ: Watford South Junction.

PASSENGER TRAIN JOURNEY TIMES (BEST TIMES IN MINUTES)[1]

Date[3]		1903	1920	1931	1939	1958	1980	2000
Distance	From Marylebone to:							
9.3 m	Harrow	15	14	14	12	14	12	11
17.2 m	Rickmansworth	–	29	26	27	27	24	21
23.6 m	Amersham	–	54	39	46	42	35	29
37.4 m	Aylesbury	53	53	52	48	59	58	49
44.3 m	Quainton Road	–	83	74	79	96	–	–
50.3 m	Verney Junction	–	106	96	–	–	–	–
	From Baker Street to:							
	Harrow	25	19	15	15	17	16	16
	Rickmansworth	42	30	30	26	31	27.5	28
18.5m	Watford	–	–[2]	33	33	39	40	37
	Amersham	59	45	53	48	50	39.5	40
	Aylesbury	87	84	72	79	80	–	–
	Quainton Road	100	90	101	90	–	–	–
	Verney Junction	119	120	131	–	–	–	–

(1) The 'best times' for each date often reflects different trains, i.e. fast v stopping.
(2) The Watford branch opened in 1925, with a Met service of 41 trains/day taking 35 mins to Baker Street and briefly an LNER service of 30 trains/day to Marylebone.
(3) Baker Street trains:
Met steam haulage beyond Harrow until 1925 and thence from Rickmansworth after electrification. LT continued with LNER locomotives until electrification to Amersham in 1961. This became the terminus for LT trains.
Marylebone trains:
Steam hauled by the GCR until 1923, thence by LNER to 1947 and after by BR until they introduced dmu's in 1960. From 1992 the Chiltern Turbos took over.

TRAIN FREQUENCY (TYPICAL NO. DOWN TRAINS ON A WEEKDAY)

Date[3]	1903	1920	1931	1939	1958	1980	2000
No. of down trains per weekday beyond Rickmansworth:							
GC/LNE/BR/Chiltern	17	23	25	28	22	19	33
Met/LT	22	23	20	28	33	33	56
No. of down trains per weekday to Watford:							
Met/LT	–	–[2]	45	54	55	69	83

REFERENCES

PRIMARY SOURCES

The main archives relating to the Joint have been transferred from the British Rail Archives to the London Metropolitan Archive at 40 Northampton Road, London, EC1R 0HB, and the following from Accession No. 1297 have been referred to in researching this book:

MGCJ 1/1	Joint Committee Minutes (written)	1906–17
MGCJ 1/2	Joint Committee Minutes (written)	1917–33
MGCJ 1/3	Joint Committee Minutes (written)	1933–48
MGCJ 1/4	Joint Committee Minutes (printed)	1906–11
MGCJ 1/5	Joint Committee Minutes (printed)	1911–22
MGCJ 1/6	Officers Conference Minutes (printed)	1906–13
MGCJ 1/7	Officers Conference Minutes (printed)	1914–36
MGCJ 1/8	Oxford & Aylesbury Tramway Co. papers	1899–1905
MGJC 3/1	Litho. plans of the Met & GC Joint Line	1907
MET 3/1	MS&LR and Met Agreements	1894–1913
MET 3/3	Acquisition of the A&BR by the Met	1899
MET 4/8	GCR use of the Met lines	1894–98
MET 4/11&13	Collection of Met printed matter & photos	----
MET 10 /39	St John's Wood Railway widening	1865–78
MET 10/42	Extension from Pinner to Rickmansworth	1885
MET 10/47	Extension from Rickmansworth to Chesham	1889
MET 10/54	Proposed extension to High Wycombe	1892–96
MET 10/112	Alterations to Harrow Station	1907–8
MET 10/126	Crash at Aylesbury Station	1904
MET 10/127	Met Pullman cars	1909–22
MET 10/230	Watford branch opening	1925
MET 10/378	Advice from Counsel	1925
MET 10/535	Opening to Aylesbury	1892
MET 10/543	Goods working	1927
MET 10/656	Trials MS&LR locomotives	1897
MET 10/659	SER, MS&LR and Met Agreements	1889–90
MET 10/700	Temporary MS&LR junction near West Hampstead	1895
MET 10/705	Discussions on division of receipts with LNER	1923
MET 10/708	Watford branch correspondence.	1931
MET 10/709	MS&LR and Met letters on gradients & clearances	1897–8
MET 10/711	Proposed extension to 'Central England'	1889
MET 10/712	Alterations to Harrow Station	1928–33
MET 10/727	Speed of GCR trains	1904
MET 10/758	LT Bill	1932
MET 15/1	Absorption of Met staff by the LTPB	1928–33
MET 19/1	Guide to the Extension	----
WAT 1/1	Watford Joint Committee Minutes	1926–47

Plus various public & working timetables, railway publications, local newspapers and other records.

SECONDARY SOURCES

Atkins, Tony (2007), *GWR Goods Services*, Wild Swan

Bailey, Keith (2008), *Aylesbury: A County Town & its Station 1877-1905*, Buckinghamshire Archaeological Society

Barker, Robert (1986), *The Metropolitan Railway and the making of Neasden*, Transport History/Brent Leisure

Barman, Christian (1979), *The Man Who Built London Transport*, David & Charles

Bloxsom, M. & Hendry, R. (1996), 'Great Central – The Real Problem', *Back Track*, vol.10, p.266

Brooksbank, B.W. L. (2007), *London Main Line War Damage*, Capital Transport

Cockman, Frank (2006), *The Railways of Buckinghamshire from the 1830s* (ed. David Thorpe), Buckinghamshire Archaeological Society

Dow, George (1959), *The Great Central Railway*, vols 1-3, Locomotive Publishing Co.

Emblin, R. & Longbone, B. (1995), 'Money Sunk & Lost', *Back Track*, vol.9, p.129

Gleick, James (1987), *Chaos: Making a New Science*, Cardinal

Goudie, Frank (1990), *Metropolitan Steam Locomotives*, Capital Transport

Greaves, Canon John (2005), *Sir Edward Watkin*, The Book Guild

Halliday, Stephen (2002), *Underground to Everywhere*, Sutton

Jackson, Alan A. (1986), *London's Metropolitan Railway*, David & Charles

Quartermaine, G.F. (1941), 'The Tickets of the Metropolitan Railway', *The Railway Magazine*, vol.87, p.542

Waywell, Robin *Industrial Locomotives of Buckinghamshire, Bedfordshire and Northamptonshire*, Industrial Locomotive Society

Wolmar, Christian (2007), *Fire & Steam (How the Railways Transformed Britain)*, Atlantic Books

INDEX

Visit our website and discover thousands of other History Press books.

www.thehistorypress.co.uk